Informing the legislative debate since 1914

# China's Economic Rise: History, Trends, Challenges, and Implications for the United States

Wayne M. Morrison

Specialist in Asian Trade and Finance

February 3, 2014

Congressional Research Service

7-5700

www.crs.gov

RL33534

# Summary

Prior to the initiation of economic reforms and trade liberalization 34 years ago, China maintained policies that kept the economy very poor, stagnant, centrally controlled, vastly inefficient, and relatively isolated from the global economy. Since opening up to foreign trade and investment and implementing free market reforms in 1979, China has been among the world's fastest-growing economies, with real annual gross domestic product (GDP) growth averaging nearly 10% through 2013. In recent years, China has emerged as a major global economic and trade power. It is currently the world's second-largest economy, largest trading economy, second-largest destination of foreign direct investment (FDI), largest manufacturer, and largest holder of foreign exchange reserves.

The global economic crisis that began in 2008 greatly affected China's economy. China's exports, imports, and FDI inflows declined, GDP growth slowed, and millions of Chinese workers reportedly lost their jobs. The Chinese government responded by implementing a $586 billion economic stimulus package, loosening monetary policies to increase bank lending, and providing various incentives to boost domestic consumption. Such policies enabled China to effectively weather the effects of the sharp global fall in demand for Chinese products, while several of the world's leading economies experienced negative or stagnant economic growth. From 2008 to 2011, China's real GDP growth averaged 9.6%. However, the economy has shown signs of slowing in recent years. Real GDP grew by 7.7% in both 2012 and 2013.

Some economists forecast that China will overtake the United States as the world's largest economy within a few years. However, the ability of China to maintain a rapidly growing economy in the long run will depend largely on the ability of the Chinese government to implement comprehensive economic reforms that more quickly hasten China's transition to a free market economy; rebalance the Chinese economy by making consumer demand, rather than exporting and fixed investment, the main engine of economic growth; boost productivity and innovation; address growing income disparities; and enhance environmental protection. The Chinese government has acknowledged that its current economic growth model needs to be altered and has announced several initiatives to address various economic challenges. In November 2013, the Communist Party of China held the Third Plenum of its 18th Party Congress, which issued a communique outlining a number of broad policy statements on reforms that would be implemented by 2020. Many of the proposed reforms are measures that would seek to boost competition and economic efficiency. For example, the communique stated that the market would now play a "decisive" role in allocating resources in the economy.

China's economic rise has significant implications for the United States and hence is of major interest to Congress. On the one hand, China is a large (and potentially huge) export market for the United States. Many U.S. firms use China as the final point of assembly in their global supply chain networks. China's large holdings of U.S. Treasury securities help the federal government finance its budget deficits. However, some analysts contend that China maintains a number of distortive economic policies (such as protectionist industrial policies and an undervalued currency) that undermine U.S. economic interests. They warn that efforts by the Chinese government to promote indigenous innovation, often through the use of subsidies and other distortive measures, could negatively affect many leading U.S. industries. This report surveys the rise of China's economy, describes major economic challenges facing China, and discusses the implications of China's economic rise for the United States.

# Contents

# Figures

## Tables

## Contacts

T he rapid rise of China as a major economic power within a time span of about three decades is often described by analysts as one of the greatest economic success stories in modern times. From 1979 (when economic reforms began) to 2013, China's real gross domestic product (GDP) grew at an average annual rate of nearly 10%.[1] It is estimated that to date 500 million people in China have been raised out of extreme poverty. China has emerged as a major global economic power. It is now the world's largest manufacturer, merchandise exporter, and holder of foreign exchange reserves. China is currently the second-largest economy after the United States, and some analysts predict that it could become the largest within the next five years or so. On a per capita basis (a common measurement of a nation's standard of living), however, China is significantly less developed than the United States.

China's rapid economic growth has led to a substantial increase in bilateral commercial ties with the United States. According to U.S. trade data, total trade between the two countries grew from $5 billion in 1980 to an estimated $558 billion in 2013. China is currently the United States' second-largest trading partner, its third-largest export market, and its largest source of imports. Many U.S. companies have extensive operations in China in order to sell their products in the booming Chinese market and to take advantage of lower-cost labor for export-oriented manufacturing.[2] These operations have helped some U.S. firms to remain internationally competitive and have supplied U.S. consumers with a variety of low-cost goods. China's large-scale purchases of U.S. Treasury securities (which totaled $1.3 trillion as of November 2013) have enabled the federal government to fund its budget deficits, which help keep U.S. interest rates relatively low.[3]

However, the emergence of China as a major economic power has raised concern among many U.S. policy makers. Some claim that China uses unfair trade practices (such as an undervalued currency and subsidies given to domestic producers) to flood U.S. markets with low-cost goods, and that such practices threaten American jobs, wages, and living standards. Others contend that China's growing use of industrial policies to promote and protect certain domestic Chinese industries firms favored by the government, and its failure to take effective action against widespread infringement of U.S. intellectual property rights (IPR) in China, threaten to undermine the competitiveness of U.S. IP-intensive industries. In addition, while China has become a large and growing market for U.S. exports, critics contend that numerous trade and investment barriers limit opportunities for U.S. firms to sell in China, or force them to set up production facilities in China as the price of doing business there. Other concerns relating to China's economic growth include its growing demand for energy and raw materials and its emergence as the world's largest emitter of greenhouse gasses.

The Chinese government views a growing economy as vital to maintaining social stability. However, China faces a number of major economic challenges which could dampen future growth, including distortive economic policies that have resulted in over-reliance on fixed investment and exports for economic growth (rather than on consumer demand), government support for state-owned firms, a weak banking system, widening income gaps, growing pollution,

---

[1] China's economic reform process began in December 1978 when the Third Plenum of the Eleventh Central Committee of the Communist Party adopted Deng Xiaoping's economic proposals. Implementation of the reforms began in 1979.

[2] Some companies use China as part of their global supply chain for manufactured parts, which are then exported and assembled elsewhere. Other firms have shifted the production of finished products from other countries (mainly in Asia) to China; they import parts and materials into China for final assembly.

[3] See CRS Report RL33536, *China-U.S. Trade Issues*, by Wayne M. Morrison.

and the relative lack of the rule of law in China. The Chinese government has acknowledged these problems and has pledged to address them by implementing policies to boost consumer spending, expand social safety net coverage, and encourage the development of less-polluting industries.

This report provides background on China's economic rise; describes its current economic structure; identifies the challenges China faces to maintain economic growth; and discusses the challenges, opportunities, and implications of China's economic rise for the United States.

# The History of China's Economic Development

## China's Economy Prior to Reforms

Prior to 1979, China, under the leadership of Chairman Mao Zedong, maintained a centrally planned, or command, economy. A large share of the country's economic output was directed and controlled by the state, which set production goals, controlled prices, and allocated resources throughout most of the economy. During the 1950s, all of China's individual household farms were collectivized into large communes. To support rapid industrialization, the central government undertook large-scale investments in physical and human capital during the 1960s and 1970s. As a result, by 1978 nearly three-fourths of industrial production was produced by centrally controlled, state-owned enterprises (SOEs), according to centrally planned output targets. Private enterprises and foreign-invested firms were generally barred. A central goal of the Chinese government was to make China's economy relatively self-sufficient. Foreign trade was generally limited to obtaining only those goods that could not be made or obtained in China.

Government policies kept the Chinese economy relatively stagnant and inefficient, mainly because most aspects of the economy were managed and run by the central government (and thus there were few profit incentives for firms, workers, and farmers), competition was virtually nonexistent, foreign trade and investment flows were mainly limited to Soviet bloc countries, and price and production controls caused widespread distortions in the economy. Chinese living standards were substantially lower than those of many other developing countries. The Chinese government in 1978 (shortly after the death of Chairman Mao in 1976) decided to break with its Soviet-style economic policies by gradually reforming the economy according to free market principles and opening up trade and investment with the West, in the hope that this would significantly increase economic growth and raise living standards. As Chinese leader Deng Xiaoping, the architect of China's economic reforms, put it: "Black cat, white cat, what does it matter what color the cat is as long as it catches mice?"[4]

## The Introduction of Economic Reforms

Beginning in 1979, China launched several economic reforms. The central government initiated price and ownership incentives for farmers, which enabled them to sell a portion of their crops on the free market. In addition, the government established four special economic zones along the coast for the purpose of attracting foreign investment, boosting exports, and importing high

---

[4] This reference appears to have meant that it did not matter whether an economic policy was considered to be "capitalist" or "socialist," what really mattered was whether that policy would boost the economy.

technology products into China. Additional reforms, which followed in stages, sought to decentralize economic policymaking in several sectors, especially trade. Economic control of various enterprises was given to provincial and local governments, which were generally allowed to operate and compete on free market principles, rather than under the direction and guidance of state planning. In addition, citizens were encouraged to start their own businesses. Additional coastal regions and cities were designated as open cities and development zones, which allowed them to experiment with free market reforms and to offer tax and trade incentives to attract foreign investment. In addition, state price controls on a wide range of products were gradually eliminated. Trade liberalization was also a major key to China's economic success. Removing trade barriers encouraged greater competition and attracted foreign direct investment (FDI) inflows. China's gradual implementation of economic reforms sought to identify which policies produced favorable economic outcomes (and which did not) so that they could be implemented in other parts of the country, a process Deng Xiaoping reportedly referred to as "crossing the river by touching the stones."[5]

## China's Economic Growth and Reforms: 1979-the Present

Since the introduction of economic reforms, China's economy has grown substantially faster than during the pre-reform period. According to the Chinese government, from 1953 to 1978, real annual GDP growth was estimated at 6.7%,[6] although many analysts claim that Chinese economic data during this period are highly questionable because government officials often exaggerated production levels for a variety of political reasons.[7] Economist Agnus Maddison estimated China's average annual real GDP during this period at 4.4%.[8]

China's economy suffered economic downturns during the leadership of Chairman Mao Zedong, including during the Great Leap Forward from 1958 to 1960 (which led to a massive famine and reportedly the deaths of tens of millions of people) and the Cultural Revolution from 1966 to 1976 (which caused political chaos and greatly disrupted the economy). Since 1979, China's average annual real GDP has grown by nearly 10% (see **Figure 1**). This has meant that, on average, China has been able to double the size of its economy in real terms every eight years.

The global economic slowdown, which began in 2008, impacted the Chinese economy (especially the export sector). China's real GDP growth fell from 14.2% in 2007 to 9.6% in 2008, and slowed to 9.2% in 2009. In response, the Chinese government implemented a large economic stimulus package and an expansive monetary policy. These measures boosted domestic investment and consumption and helped prevent a sharp economic slowdown in China. From 2009 to 2011, China's real GDP growth averaged 9.6%. China's economy has slowed in recent years—real GDP

---

[5] Many analysts contend that Deng's push to implement economic reforms was largely motivated by a belief that the resulting economic growth would ensure that the Communist Party stayed in power.

[6] Chinability, *GDP Growth in China, 1952-2011*, at http://www.chinability.com/GDP htm.

[7] During the Great Leap Forward, local Chinese officials are believed to have often exaggerated agricultural production to prove their ability to implement Mao's economic policies in order to advance their careers or to avoid getting into political trouble with Beijing. Central government officials may have also exaggerated China's economic statistics in order to illustrate the "success" of the government's economic policies.

[8] The Organization for Economic Cooperation and Development, *Chinese Economic Performance in the Long Run, 960-2030*, by Angus Maddison, 2007.

grew by 7.7 in 2012 and 2013. The International Monetary Fund (IMF) has projected that China's real GDP growth will average 7.0% from 2014 to 2018.[9]

**Figure 1. Chinese Real GDP Growth: 1979-2013**

(percent)

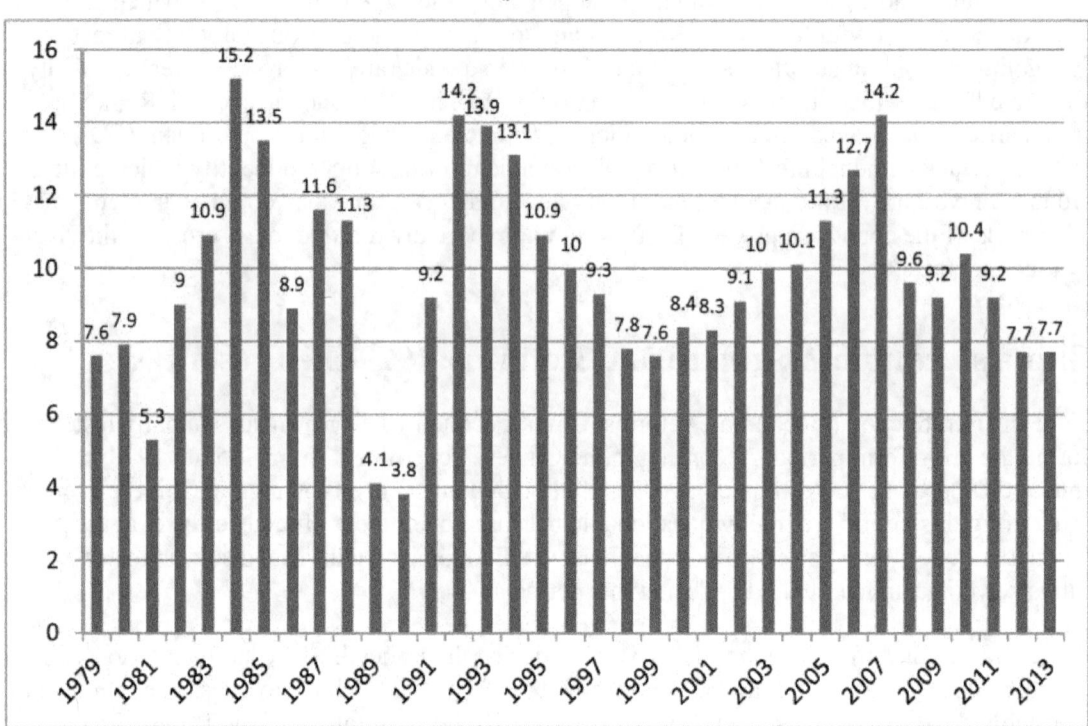

**Source:** Economist Intelligence Unit and official Chinese government data.

## Causes of China's Economic Growth

Economists generally attribute much of China's rapid economic growth to two main factors: large-scale capital investment (financed by large domestic savings and foreign investment) and rapid productivity growth. These two factors appear to have gone together hand in hand. Economic reforms led to higher efficiency in the economy, which boosted output and increased resources for additional investment in the economy.

China has historically maintained a high rate of savings. When reforms were initiated in 1979, domestic savings as a percentage of GDP stood at 32%. However, most Chinese savings during this period were generated by the profits of SOEs, which were used by the central government for domestic investment. Economic reforms, which included the decentralization of economic production, led to substantial growth in Chinese household savings as well as corporate savings. As a result, China's gross savings as a percentage of GDP is the highest among major economies. The large level of savings has enabled China to substantially boost domestic investment. In fact,

---

[9] IMF, *World Economic Outlook Database*, October 2013.

China's gross domestic savings levels far exceed its domestic investment levels, which have made China a large net global lender.

Several economists have concluded that productivity gains (i.e., increases in efficiency) have been another major factor in China's rapid economic growth. The improvements to productivity were caused largely by a reallocation of resources to more productive uses, especially in sectors that were formerly heavily controlled by the central government, such as agriculture, trade, and services. For example, agricultural reforms boosted production, freeing workers to pursue employment in the more productive manufacturing sector. China's decentralization of the economy led to the rise of non-state enterprises (such as private firms), which tended to pursue more productive activities than the centrally-controlled SOEs and were more market-oriented and more efficient. Additionally, a greater share of the economy (mainly the export sector) was exposed to competitive forces. Local and provincial governments were allowed to establish and operate various enterprises without interference from the government. In addition, FDI in China brought with it new technology and processes that boosted efficiency.

However, as China's technological development begins to approach that of major developed countries (i.e., through its adsorption of foreign technology), its level of productivity gains, and thus, real GDP growth, could slow significantly from its historic levels unless China is become a major center for new technology and innovation and/or implements new comprehensive economic reforms. Several developing economies (notably several in Asia and Latin America) experienced rapid economic development and growth during the 1960s and 1970s by implementing some of the same policies that China has utilized to date to develop its economy, such as measures to boost exports and to promote and protect certain industries. However, at some point in their development, some of these countries began to experience economic stagnation (or much slower growth compared to previous levels) over a sustained period of time, a phenomenon described by economists as the "middle-income trap."[10] This means that several developing (low-income) economies were able to transition to a middle income economy, but because they were unable to sustain high levels of productivity gains (in part because they could not address structural inefficiencies in the economy), they were unable to transition to a high-income economy.[11] China may be at a similar crossroads now.[12] The Economist Intelligence Unit (EIU) projects that China's real GDP growth will slow considerably in the years ahead, averaging 6.3% from 2014 to 2020, and 3.7% from 2021 to 2030 (**Figure 2**).[13]

The Chinese government has indicated its desire to move away from its current economic model of fast growth at any cost to more "smart" economic growth, which seeks to reduce reliance on energy-intensive and high-polluting industries and rely more on high technology, green energy, and services. China also has indicated it wants to obtain more balanced economic growth. (These issues are discussed in more detail later in the report.)

---

[10] Japan was able to become a high-income economy, but since the mid-1980s, its economic growth has been relatively stagnant. See CRS Report RL30176, *Japan's "Economic Miracle": What Happened?*, by William H. Cooper.

[11] These designations are based on World Bank per capita GDP measurements.

[12] For a discussion of this issue, see the World Bank, China 2030, 2013, p. 12, at http://www-wds.worldbank.org/external/default/WDSContentServer/WDSP/IB/2013/03/27/000350881_20130327163105/Rendered/PDF/762990PUB0china0Box374372B00PUBLIC0.pdf.

[13] Note, long-term economic projections should be viewed with caution.

**Figure 2. Projections of U.S. and Chinese Annual Real GDP Growth Rates: 2014-2030**

(percent)

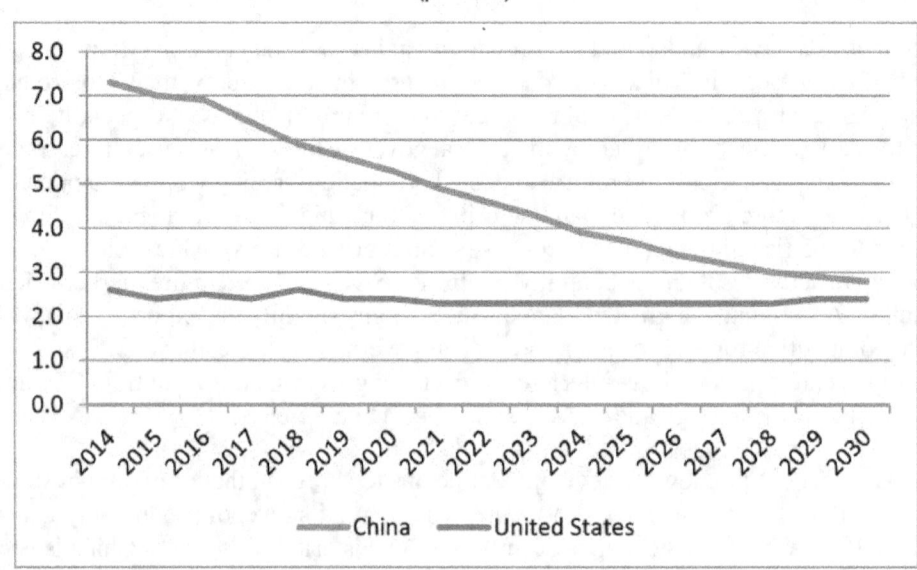

**Source:** Economist Intelligence Unit.

**Note:** Long-range economic projections should be viewed with caution.

# Measuring the Size of China's Economy

The rapid growth of the Chinese economy has led many analysts to speculate if and when China will overtake the United States as the "world's largest economic power." The "actual" size of China's economy has been a subject of extensive debate among economists. Measured in U.S. dollars using nominal exchange rates, China's GDP in 2012 was $9.4 trillion, about 56% the size of the U.S. economy.[14] The per capita GDP (a common measurement of a country's living standards) of China was $6,960, which was 17.8% the size of Japan's level and 13.1% that of the United States (see **Table 1**).

Many economists contend that using nominal exchange rates to convert Chinese data (or that of other countries) into U.S. dollars fails to reflect the true size of China's economy and living standards relative to the United States. Nominal exchange rates simply reflect the prices of foreign currencies vis-à-vis the U.S. dollar and such measurements exclude differences in the prices for goods and services across countries. To illustrate, one U.S. dollar exchanged for local currency in China would buy more goods and services there than it would in the United States. This is because prices for goods and services in China are generally lower than they are in the United States. Conversely, prices for goods and services in Japan are generally higher than they are in the United States (and China). Thus, one dollar exchanged for local Japanese currency would buy fewer goods and services there than it would in the United States. Economists attempt to develop estimates of exchange rates based on their actual purchasing power relative to the

---

[14] On a nominal dollar basis, China overtook Japan in 2010 to become the world's second-largest economy (after the United States).

dollar in order to make more accurate comparisons of economic data across countries, usually referred to as purchasing power parity (PPP).

The PPP exchange rate increases the (estimated) measurement of China's economy and its per capita GDP. According to the EIU, which uses World Bank data, prices for goods and services in China are about 45% the level they are in the United States. Adjusting for this price differential raises the value of China's 2013 GDP from $9.4 trillion (nominal dollars) to $13.6 trillion (on a PPP basis).[15] This would indicate that China's economy is 80.9% the size of the U.S. economy. China's share of global GDP on a PPP basis rose from 3.7% in 1990 to 15.4% in 2013 (the U.S. share of global GDP peaked at 24.3% in 1999 and declined to 19.0% in 2013).

Many economic analysts predict that on a PPP basis China will soon overtake the United States as the world's largest economy. EIU, for example, projects this could occur by 2019 (see **Figure 3**), and that by 2030, China's economy could be 18.6% larger than that of the United States.[16] This would not be the first time in history that China was the world's largest economy (see text box).

---

### The Decline and Rise of China's Economy

According to a study by economist Angus Maddison, China was the world's largest economy in 1820, accounting for an estimated 32.9% of global GDP. However, foreign and civil wars, internal strife, weak and ineffective governments, natural disasters (some of which were man-made), and distortive economic policies caused China's share of global GDP on a PPP basis to shrink significantly. By 1952, China's share of global GDP had fallen to 5.2%, and by 1978, it slid to 4.9%.[17] The adoption of economic reforms by China in the late 1970s led to a surge in China's economic growth and has helped restore China as a major global economic power.

**Source:** The Organization for Economic Cooperation and Development, *Chinese Economic Performance in the Long Run, 960-2030*, by Angus Maddison, 2007.

---

The PPP measurement also raises China's 2013 nominal per capita GDP (from $6,960) to $10,060, which was 19.0% of the U.S. level. The EIU projects that, even by the year 2030, U.S. living standards will be three times greater than those in China. Thus, although China could become the world's largest economy in a few years on a PPP basis, it will likely take many years for its living standards to approach U.S. levels.[18]

### Table 1. Comparisons of Chinese, Japanese, and U.S. GDP and Per Capita GDP in Nominal U.S. Dollars and a Purchasing Power Parity Basis: 2013

|  | China | Japan | United States |
|---|---|---|---|
| Nominal GDP ($ billions) | 9,394 | 4,907 | 16,786 |
| GDP in PPP ($ billions) | 13,579 | 4,618 | 16,786 |
| Nominal Per Capita GDP ($) | 6,960 | 39,040 | 53,060 |
| Per Capita GDP in PPP ($) | 10,060 | 36,740 | 53,060 |

**Source:** Economist Intelligence Unit estimates using World Bank PPP data.

---

[15] In other words, the PPP data reflect what the value of China's goods and services would be if they were sold in the United States.

[16] However, such long-term economic projections should be viewed with caution.

[17] In comparison, the U.S. share of global GDP was estimated to have risen from 1.8% in 1820 to 27.5% in 1952, but declined to 21.6% by 1978.

[18] EIU database, surveyed on February 3, 2014.

**Figure 3. Projections for Chinese and U.S. GDP on a PPP Basis: 2014-2030**

($ trillions)

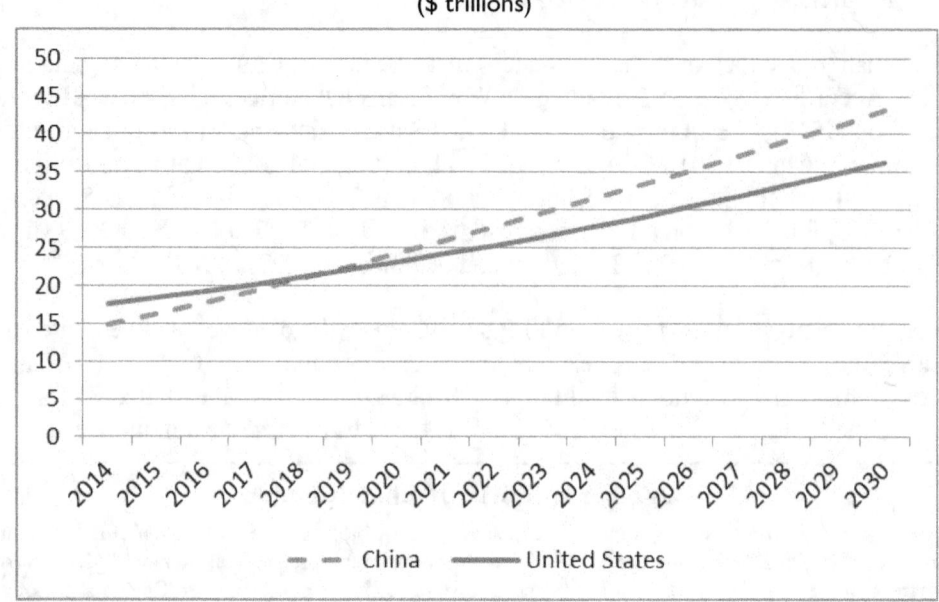

**Source:** Economist Intelligence Unit.

**Note:** Long-term economic projections should be viewed with caution.

## China as the World's Largest Manufacturer

China has emerged as the world's largest manufacturer according to the United Nations. **Figure 4** lists estimates of the gross value added of manufacturing in China, the United States, and Japan expressed in U.S. dollars for 2004 to 2012. Gross value added data reflect the actual value of manufacturing that occurred in the country (i.e., they subtract the value of intermediate inputs and raw materials used in production). These data indicate that China overtook Japan as the world's second-largest manufacturer on a gross value added basis in 2006 and the United States in 2010. In 2012, the value of China's manufacturing on a gross value added basis was 28.2% higher than that in the United States. Manufacturing plays a considerably more important role in the Chinese economy than it does for the United States and Japan. In 2011, China's gross valued added manufacturing was equal to 30.5% of GDP, compared to 12.3% for the United States and 18.7% for Japan.[19]

In its 2013 Global Manufacturing Competitiveness Index, Deloitte (an international consulting firm) ranked China first in manufacturing in 2013 and projected it would remain so in five years (the United States ranked third in 2013 and was projected to rank fifth in 2018). The report stated that "China's competitiveness is bolstered by conducive policy environment either encouraging or directly funding investments in science and technology, employee education and infrastructure development," and further stated that "the landscape for competitive manufacturing is in the midst of a massive power shift, in which twentieth-century manufacturing stalwarts like the

---

[19] United Nations, *UNdata*.

United States, Germany and Japan will be challenged to maintain their competitive edge to emerging nations, including China."[20]

**Figure 4. Gross Value Added Manufacturing in China, the United States, and Japan: 2004-2012**

(\$ billions)

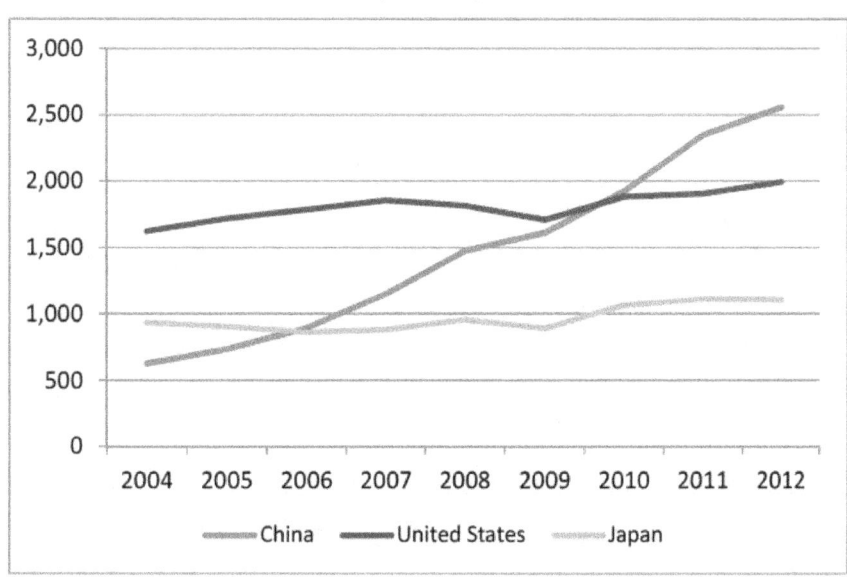

**Source:** United Nations, UNdata.

## Changes in China's Wage Advantage

China's huge population and relatively low wage rates gave it a significant competitive advantage when economic reforms and trade liberalization were first begun by the government in the late 1970s. However, this advantage appears to be eroding as wages in China have risen in recent years. From 2000 to 2013, Chinese average real wages grew at an average annual rate of 11.4%. As indicated in **Figure 5**, China's average monthly wages in 2000 were \$94 compared with \$311 per month for Mexico (China's wages were 30.2% the size of Mexican wages).[21] However, in 2013, China's average monthly wages at \$694 were 50.5% higher than those in Mexico (\$461). In 2000, China's average wages were 92% higher than those than Vietnam, but by 2013, they were 168% higher. A 2012 survey by the American Chamber of Commerce of its member companies in China reported that 39% of respondents said that labor costs ranked as the biggest business risk facing their China operations (up from 23% in 2011) and 82% stated that rising labor costs were affecting their China operations.[22] In addition, 89% of respondents said that China was losing its

---

[20] Deloitte, Press Release, January 22, 2013, available at http://www.deloitte.com/view/en_CN/cn/Pressroom/pr/105280463d16c310VgnVCM2000003356f70aRCRD.htm. The index was based on a survey of 550 chief executive officers and senior leaders in manufacturing companies around the world.

[21] Wage data are from the Economist Intelligence Unit.

[22] This issue ranked third overall among respondents as the biggest risk, after the Chinese economic slowdown and the global economic slowdown. Source: U.S. Chamber of Commerce, *2012 China Business Climate Survey Report*, March 26, 2012, p.10.

competitive edge "to some degree" or "to a great degree" due to rising costs.[23] Rising labor costs are one of the main reasons why the Chinese government has focused on boosting the nation's innovation and productivity levels.[24]

### Figure 5. Average Monthly Wages for Selected Countries: 2000-2013

(U.S. dollars)

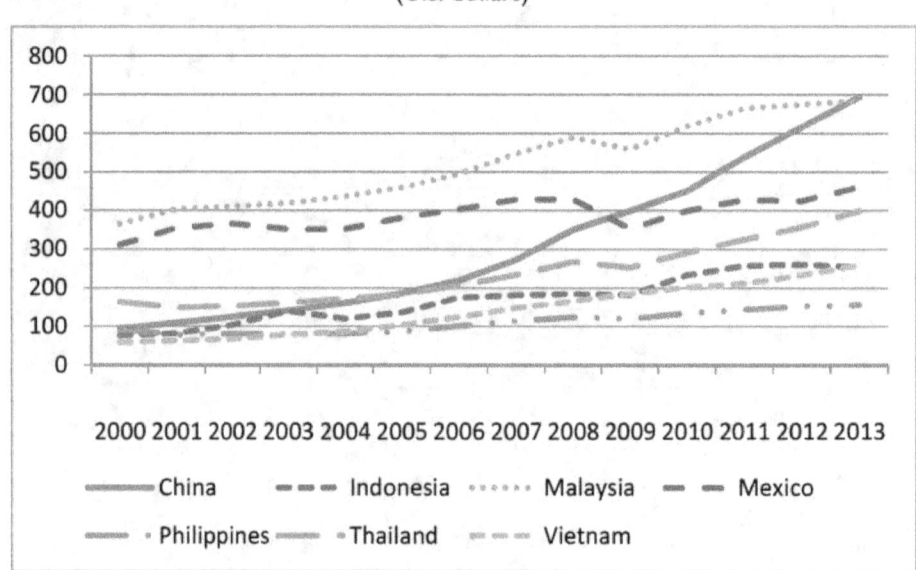

**Source:** Economist Intelligence Unit.

**Notes:** Because data are listed in U.S. dollars rather than local currency, changes to monthly wages may also partially reflect changes to exchange rates with the U.S. dollar. However, such data reflect average labor costs that U.S.-invested firms in China might face.

# Foreign Direct Investment (FDI) in China

China's trade and investment reforms and incentives led to a surge in FDI beginning in the early 1990s. Such flows have been a major source of China's productivity gains and rapid economic and trade growth. There were reportedly 445,244 foreign-invested enterprises (FIEs) registered in China in 2010, employing 55.2 million workers or 15.9% of the urban workforce.[25] As indicated in **Figure 6**, FIEs account for a significant share of China's industrial output. That level rose from 2.3% in 1990 to a high of 35.9% in 2003, but fell to 25.9% as of 2011.[26] In addition, FIEs are responsible for a significant level of China's foreign trade. In 2013, FIEs in China accounted for 47.3% of China's exports and 44.8% of its imports, although this level was down from its peak in

---

[23] Rising labor costs in China reflect a number of factors, including changing demographics in China (such as growing labor shortages), new social insurance measures, and efforts by the government to boost the minimum wage and improve working conditions, in part to boost domestic consumption.

[24] Despite rising labor costs, China continues to enjoy a significant excess supply of labor, estimated by the IMF to be currently at 150 million. However, that level is projected to fall to around 30 million by 2020. See IMF, *2012 Article IV Report, People's Republic of China*, July 2012, p.8.

[25] China 2012 Statistical Yearbook.

[26] Industrial output is defined by the Chinese government as the total volume of final industrial products produced and industrial services provided during a given period. Source: China 2012 Statistical Yearbook.

2006 when FIEs' share of Chinese exports and imports was 58.2% and 59.7%, respectively, as indicated in **Figure 7**. FIEs in China dominate China's high technology exports. From 2002 to 2010, the share of China's high tech exports by FIEs rose from 79% to 82%. During the same period, the share of China's high tech exports by wholly owned foreign firms (which excludes foreign joint ventures with Chinese firms) rose from 55% to 67%.

**Figure 6. Industrial Output by Foreign-Invested Firms in China as a Share of National Output Total: 1990-2011**

(percent)

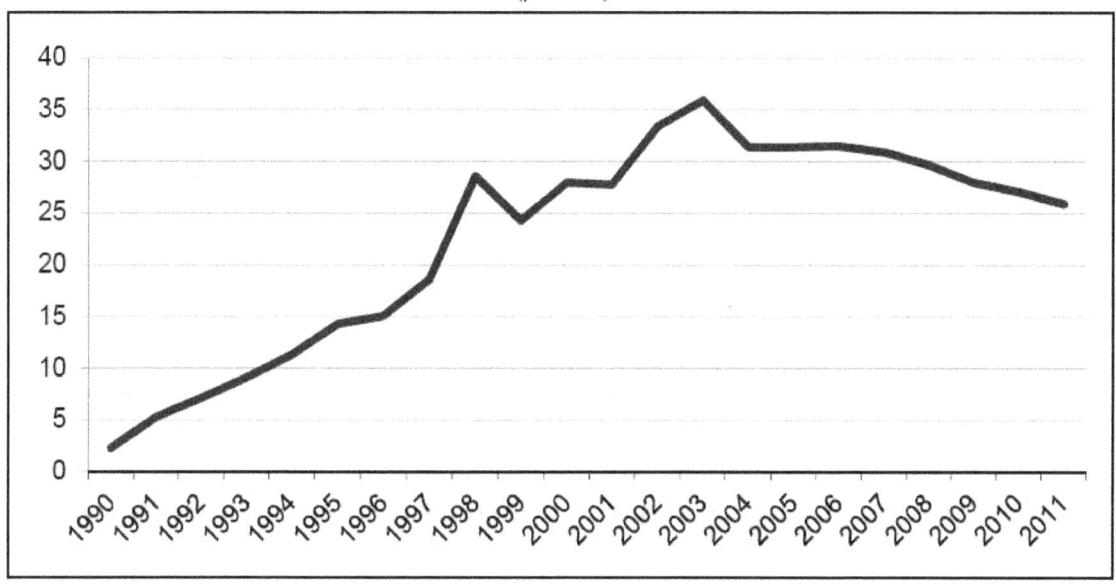

**Source:** Invest in China (http://www.fdi.gov.cn) and China's 2012 Statistical Yearbook.

**Figure 7. Share of China's Exports and Imports Attributed to Foreign-Invested Enterprises in China: 1990-2013**

(percent)

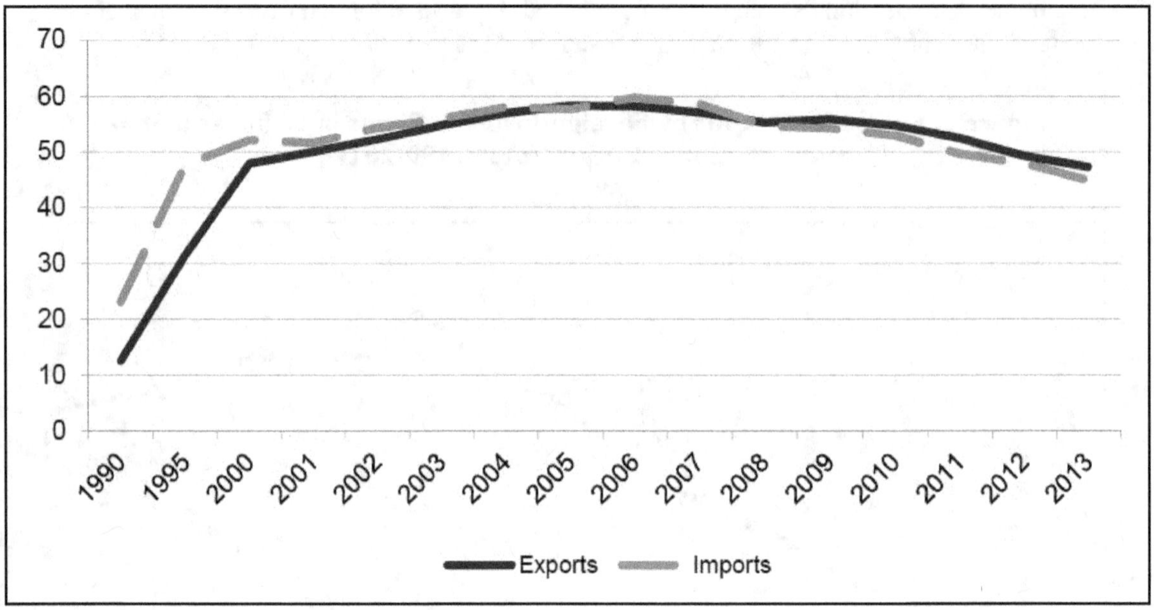

**Source:** Invest in China (http://www.fdi.gov.cn).

According to the United Nations, annual FDI flows to China grew from $2 billion 1985 to an estimated $121 billion in 2013 (see **Figure 8**), and may have reached $127 billion in 2013. The U.N. further estimates the stock of FDI in China through 2012 at $832.9 billion.[27] As indicated in **Figure 9**, China was the world's second-largest destination for FDI flows in 2012 (after the United States).[28]

According to Chinese government data on non-financial FDI inflows, the largest sources of cumulative FDI in China for 1979-2013 were Hong Kong (47.0%),[29] the British Virgin Islands BVI), Japan, the United States, and Taiwan (see **Table 2**).[30] The largest sources of non-financial FDI inflows into China in 2013 were Hong Kong (67% of total), Singapore, Japan, Taiwan, and the United States. According to Chinese data, annual U.S. non-financial FDI flows to China peaked at $5.4 billion in 2002 (10.2% of total FDI in China). In 2013, they were $3.4 billion or

---

[27] U.N. data differ from Chinese data, in part because Chinese data include only nonfinancial FDI.

[28] United Nations, *Global Investment Trends Monitor*, No. 11, January 11, 2013.

[29] Much of the FDI originating from Hong Kong may originate from other foreign investors, such as Taiwan. In addition, some Chinese investors might be using these locations to shift funds overseas in order to re-invest in China to take advantage of preferential investment policies (this practice is often referred to as "round-tipping"). Thus, the actual level of FDI in China may be overstated.

[30] Cumulative values are totals of the data collected each year, are not adjusted for inflation, and do not reflect divestment that may have occurred.

2.9% of total FDI flows to China (see **Figure 10**).[31] The stock of U.S. non-financial FDI in China (based on Chinese data) was $74.6 through 2013.[32]

### Figure 8. Annual FDI Flows to China: 1985-2013

($ billions)

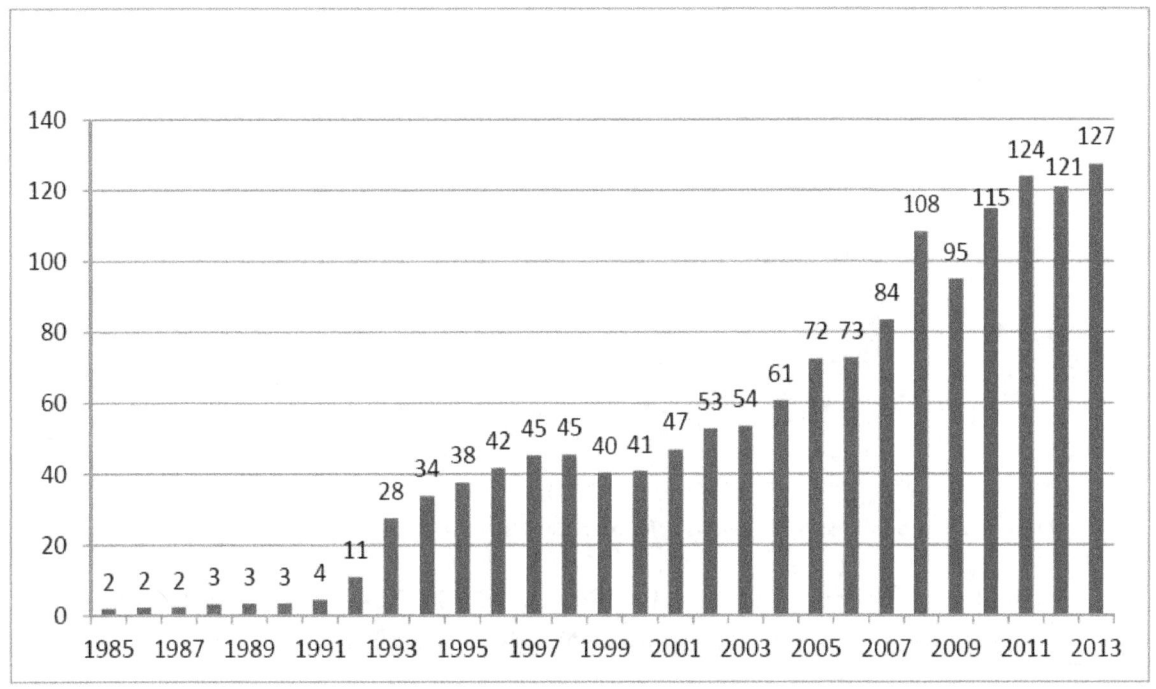

**Source:** Data for 1985-2012 are from the United Nations.

**Notes:** Data for 2013 are estimates using the Chinese Ministry of Commerce 2013 data for non-financial FDI.

---

[31] U.S. data on bilateral FDI flows with China differ significantly with Chinese data. For additional info on bilateral FDI flows based on U.S. data, see CRS Report RL33536, *China-U.S. Trade Issues*, by Wayne M. Morrison.

[32] These data are accumulated annul data on FDI flows reported by the Chinese government and do not reflect the historic-cost value of current U.S. FDI in China.

### Figure 9. Major Recipients of Global FDI Inflows in 2012

($ billions)

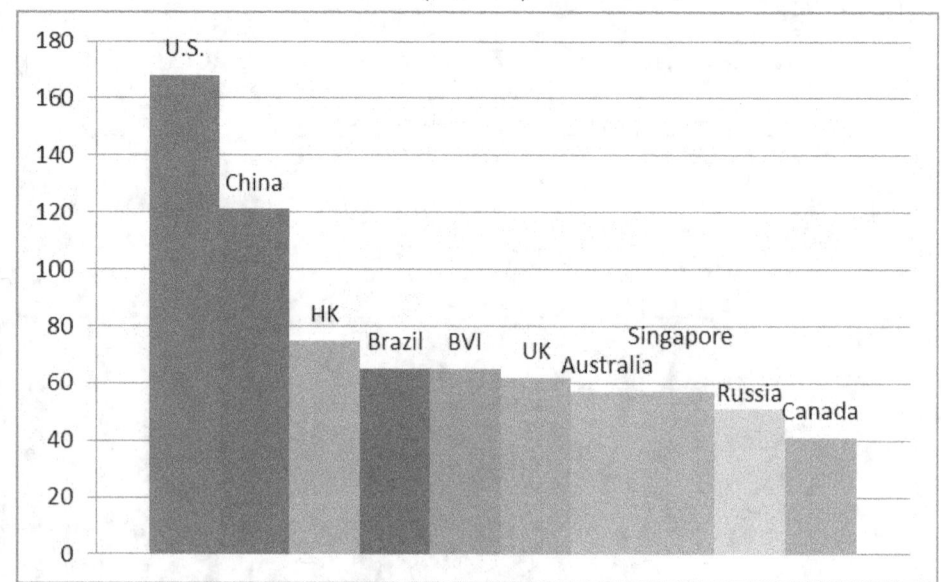

**Source:** United Nations Conference on Trade and Investment.

**Note**: U.N. data on China's FDI inflows differ from China's official data.

### Table 2. Chinese Data on Major Sources of FDI Flows to China: 1979-2013

($ billions and percentage of total)

| Country | Estimated Cumulative Utilized FDI: 1979-2013 | | Utilized FDI in 2013 | |
|---|---|---|---|---|
| | Amount | % of Total | Amount | % of Total |
| Total | 1,453.3 | 100.0 | 117.6 | 100.0 |
| Hong Kong | 682.8 | 47.0 | 78.3 | 66.6 |
| British Virgin Islands* | 111.8 | 7.7 | NA | NA |
| Japan | 94.4 | 6.5 | 7.1 | 6.0 |
| United States | 74.6 | 5.1 | 3.4 | 2.9 |
| Taiwan | 70.1 | 4.8 | 5.2 | 4.4 |
| Singapore | 67.2 | 4.6 | 7.3 | 6.2 |
| South Korea | 56.1 | 3.9 | 3.1 | 2.6 |

**Source:** Chinese Ministry of Commerce and Chinese Statistical Yearbook.

**Note:** Ranked by cumulative top seven sources of FDI in China through 2013. *Data for the British Virgin Islands are through 2010. China's cumulative data are the sum of annual data and do not reflect disinvestment or current value.

**Figure 10. Chinese Data on Annual U.S. FDI Flows to China: 1985-2013**

($ millions)

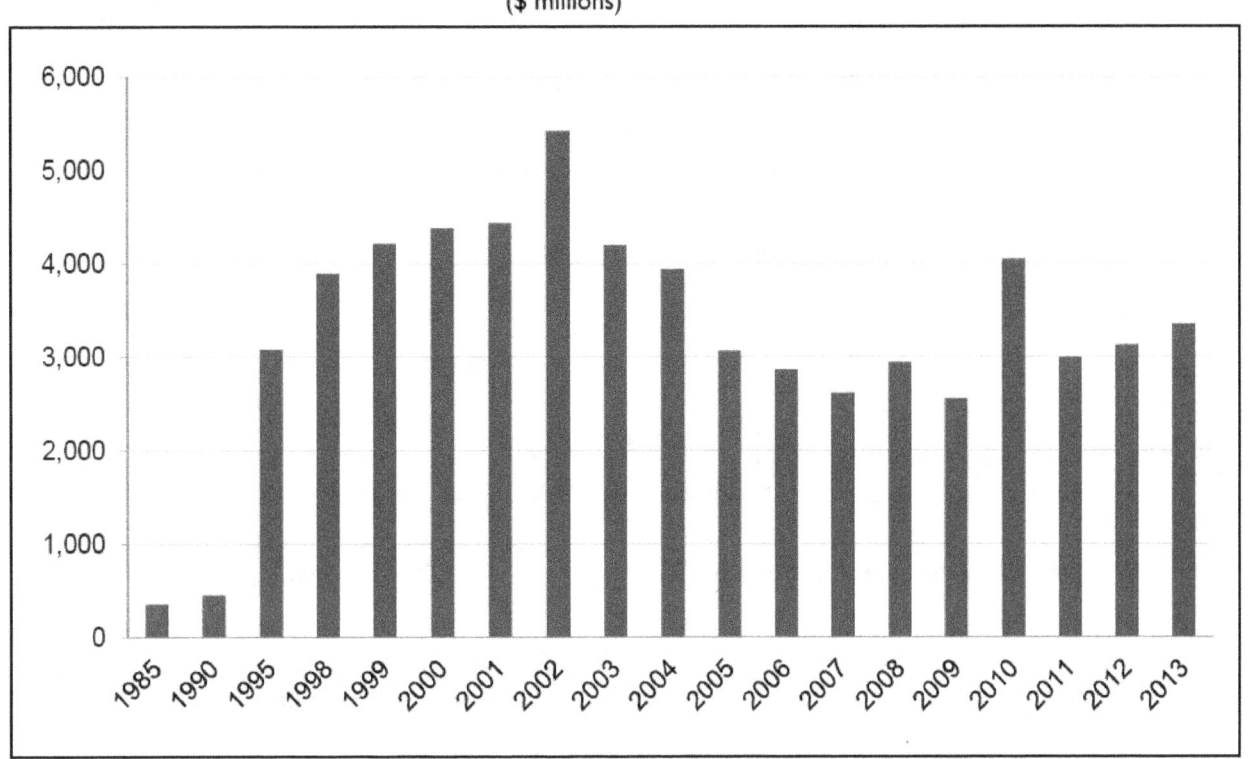

**Source:** Chinese Ministry of Commerce and Chinese Yearbook, various years.

**Note:** Chinese and U.S. data on bilateral FDI flows differ sharply because of different methodologies used. Data for 2013 are estimates, based on actual data for January-December 2013.

# China's Growing FDI Outflows

A key aspect of China's economic modernization and growth strategy during the 1980s and 1990s was to attract FDI into China to help boost the development of domestic firms. Investment by Chinese firms abroad was sharply restricted. However, in 2000, China's leaders initiated a new "go global" strategy, which sought to encourage Chinese firms (primarily SOEs) to invest overseas. One key factor driving this investment is China's massive accumulation of foreign exchange reserves. Traditionally, a significant level of those reserves has been invested in relatively safe, but low-yielding, assets, such as U.S. Treasury securities. On September 29, 2007, the Chinese government officially launched the China Investment Corporation (CIC) in an effort to seek more profitable returns on its foreign exchange reserves and diversify away from its U.S. dollar holdings. The CIC was originally funded at $200 billion, making it one of the world's largest sovereign wealth funds.[33] Another factor behind the government's drive to encourage more outward FDI flows has been to obtain natural resources, such as oil and minerals, deemed by the government as necessary to sustain China's rapid economic growth.[34] Finally, the Chinese

---

[33] See CRS Report RL34337, *China's Sovereign Wealth Fund*, by Michael F. Martin.

[34] Chinese oil and mineral companies are dominated by SOEs.

government has indicated its goal of developing globally competitive Chinese firms with their own brands. Investing in foreign firms, or acquiring them, is viewed as a method for Chinese firms to obtain technology, management skills, and often, internationally recognized brands, needed to help Chinese firms become more globally competitive. For example, in April 2005, Lenovo Group Limited, a Chinese computer company, purchased IBM Corporation's personal computer division for $1.75 billion.[35] Similarly, overseas FDI in new plants and businesses is viewed as developing multinational Chinese firms with production facilities and R&D operations around the world.

China has become a significant source of global FDI outflows, which, according to the U.N. rose from $2.7 billion in 2002 to $84.2 billion in 2012 (see **Figure 11**).[36] China ranked as the third-largest source of global FDI in 2012 (up from sixth in 2011).[37] The stock of China's outward FDI through 2012 is estimated at over $450 billion.[38] An estimate of China's FDI outflows by destination for 2012 are listed in **Table 3**. These data indicate that the largest destination of total Chinese FDI through 2012 were Hong Kong (57.5% of total), the BVI, the Cayman Islands, the United States , and Australia. In terms of Chinese FDI flows in 2012, the largest recipients were Hong Kong (58.3% of total), the United States, Kazakhstan, the United Kingdom, and the BVI.

**Table 3. Major Destinations of Chinese Overseas Direct Investment in 2012: Flows and Stock**

($billions)

| Destination | FDI Flows in 2012 | Stock of FDI through 2012 | Share of FDI Stock through 2012 (%) |
|---|---|---|---|
| Hong Kong | 51.2 | 306.0 | 57.5 |
| British Virgin Islands | 2.2 | 30.9 | 5.8 |
| Cayman Islands | 0.8 | 30.1 | 5.7 |
| United States | 4.0 | 17.1 | 3.3 |
| Australia | 2.2 | 13.9 | 2.6 |
| Singapore | 1.5 | 12.4 | 2.3 |
| Luxembourg | 1.1 | 9.0 | 1.7 |

**Source:** Estimated by BBVA Research.

**Note:** Ranked according to the top seven destinations of Chinese FDI outflows through 2012.

---

[35] The Chinese government is believed to be Lenovo's largest shareholder. For additional information on China's FDI flows to the United States, see CRS Report RL33536, *China-U.S. Trade Issues*, by Wayne M. Morrison

[36] According to Chinese government data, China's nonfinancial FDI outflows in 2013 were

[37] United Nations Conference on Trade and Development, World Investment Report 2012, June 2013.

[38] United Nations Conference on Trade and Development.

### Figure 11. China's Annual FDI Outflows: 2000-2013

($ billions)

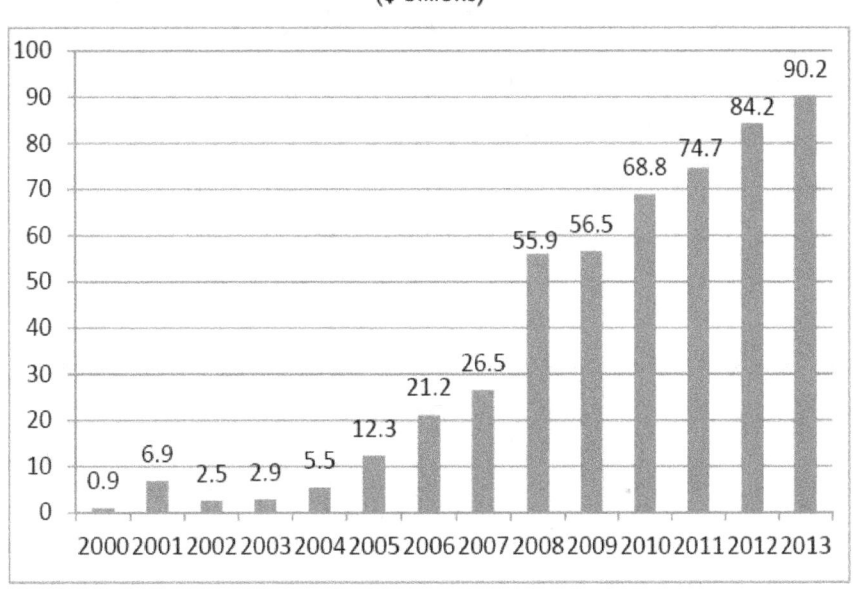

**Source:** Data for 2000-2012 are estimates made by the United Nations. Data for 2013 are from the Chinese Ministry of Commerce and exclude financial FDI outflows.

**Note:** U.N. data on Chinese FDI differ from official Chinese data.

# China's Merchandise Trade Patterns

Economic reforms and trade and investment liberalization have helped transform China into a major trading power. Chinese merchandise exports rose from $14 billion in 1979 to $2.2 trillion in 2013, while merchandise imports grew from $18 billion to $1.9 trillion (see **Table 4** and **Figure 12**).

From 1990 to 2013, the annual growth of China's exports and imports averaged 18.5% and 17.3%, respectively (see **Figure 13**).[39] China's exports and imports in 2013 grew by 7.8% and 7.3%, respectively China's merchandise trade surplus grew sharply from 2004 to 2008, rising from $32 billion to $297 billion. That surplus fell each year from 2009 to 2011, dropping to $158 billion. However, in 2012, China's trade surplus rose to $233 billion and in 2013 it increased to $261 billion.

In 2009, China overtook Germany to become both the world's largest merchandise exporter and the second-largest merchandise importer (after the United States). In 2012, China overtook the United States as the world's largest merchandise trading economy.[40] As indicated in **Figure 14**, China's share of global merchandise exports more than tripled from 2000 to 2013, rising from 3.8% to 12.1%;[41] the World Bank projects this figure could increase to 20% by 2030.[42]

---

[39] Chinese exports and imports dropped sharply in 2009 (over 2008 levels) because of the global economic slowdown. By 2010, China's trade had recovered and exceeded pre-crisis levels.

[40] In 2013, China became the largest trading economy for goods and services.

[41] Economist Intelligence Unit, *Data Tools*.

Merchandise trade surpluses, large-scale foreign investment, and large purchases of foreign currencies to maintain its exchange rate with the dollar and other currencies have enabled China to become by far the world's largest holder of foreign exchange reserves at nearly $3.7 trillion as of September 2013.

### Table 4. China's Merchandise World Trade: 1979-2013

($ billions)

| Year | Exports | Imports | Trade Balance |
| --- | --- | --- | --- |
| 1979 | 13.7 | 15.7 | −2.0 |
| 1980 | 18.1 | 19.5 | −1.4 |
| 1985 | 27.3 | 42.5 | −15.3 |
| 1990 | 62.9 | 53.9 | 9.0 |
| 1995 | 148.8 | 132.1 | 16.7 |
| 2000 | 249.2 | 225.1 | 24.1 |
| 2001 | 266.2 | 243.6 | 22.6 |
| 2002 | 325.6 | 295.2 | 30.4 |
| 2003 | 438.4 | 412.8 | 25.6 |
| 2004 | 593.4 | 561.4 | 32.0 |
| 2005 | 762.0 | 660.1 | 101.9 |
| 2006 | 969.1 | 791.5 | 177.6 |
| 2007 | 1,218.0 | 955.8 | 262.2 |
| 2008 | 1,428.9 | 1,131.5 | 297.4 |
| 2009 | 1,202.0 | 1,003.9 | 198.2 |
| 2010 | 1,578.4 | 1,393.9 | 184.5 |
| 2011 | 1,899.3 | 1,741.4 | 157.9 |
| 2012 | 2,050.1 | 1,817.3 | 232.8 |
| 2013 | 2,210.7 | 1,949.3 | 261.4 |

**Source:** *Global Trade Atlas.*

**Note:** Chinese data often differ from those of its trading partners.

---

(...continued)

[42] The World Bank, *China 2030, Building a Modern, Harmonious, and Creative High-Income Society*, 2012, p. 14. Hereinafter referred to as World Bank, *China 2030*.

### Figure 12. China's Merchandise Trade: 2000-2013

($ billions)

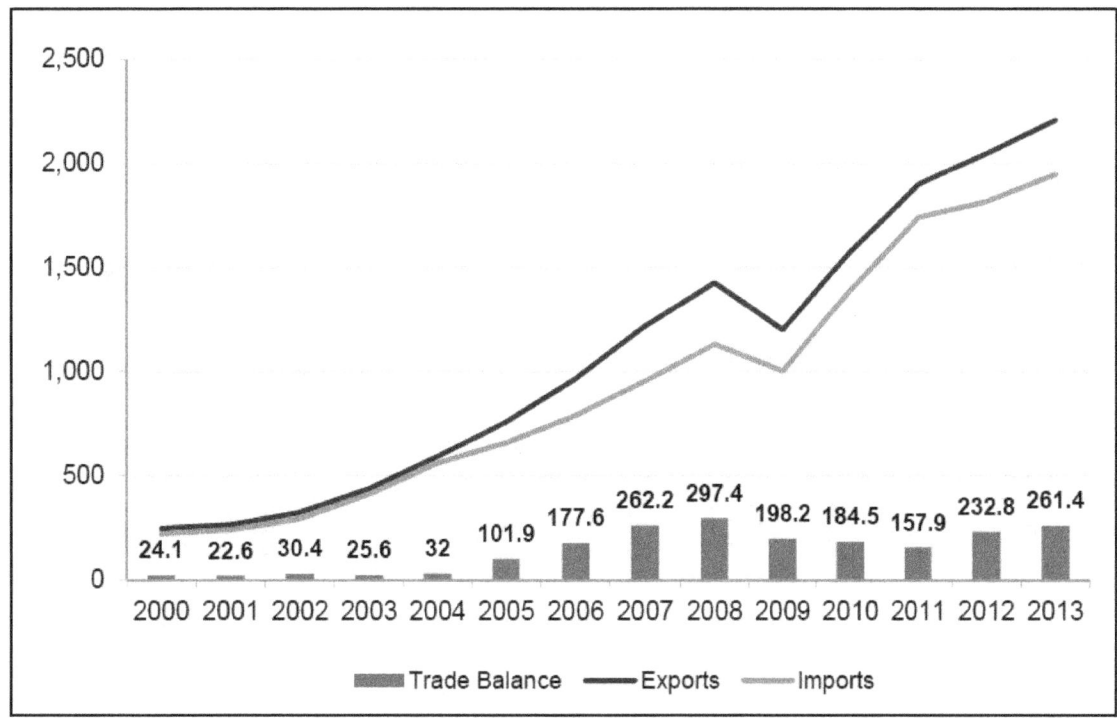

**Source:** World Trade Atlas.

**Note:** Chinese data often differ from those of its trading partners.

### Figure 13. Annual Change in China's Merchandise Exports and Imports: 1990-2013

(percent)

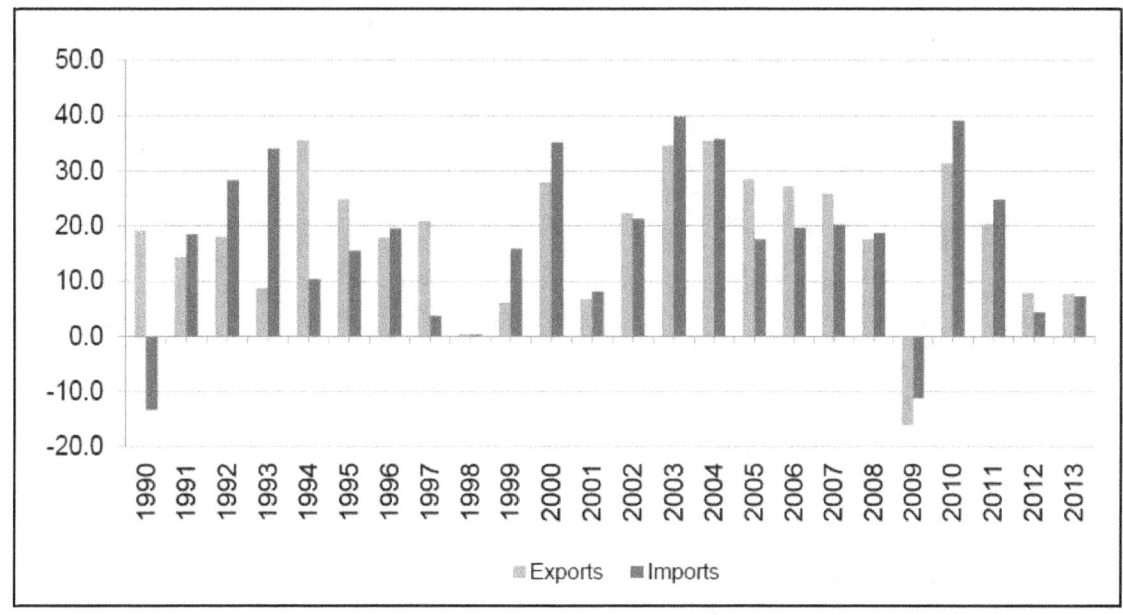

**Source:** *Global Trade Atlas* using official Chinese data.

**Figure 14. China's Share of Global Merchandise Exports: 1990-2013**

($billions)

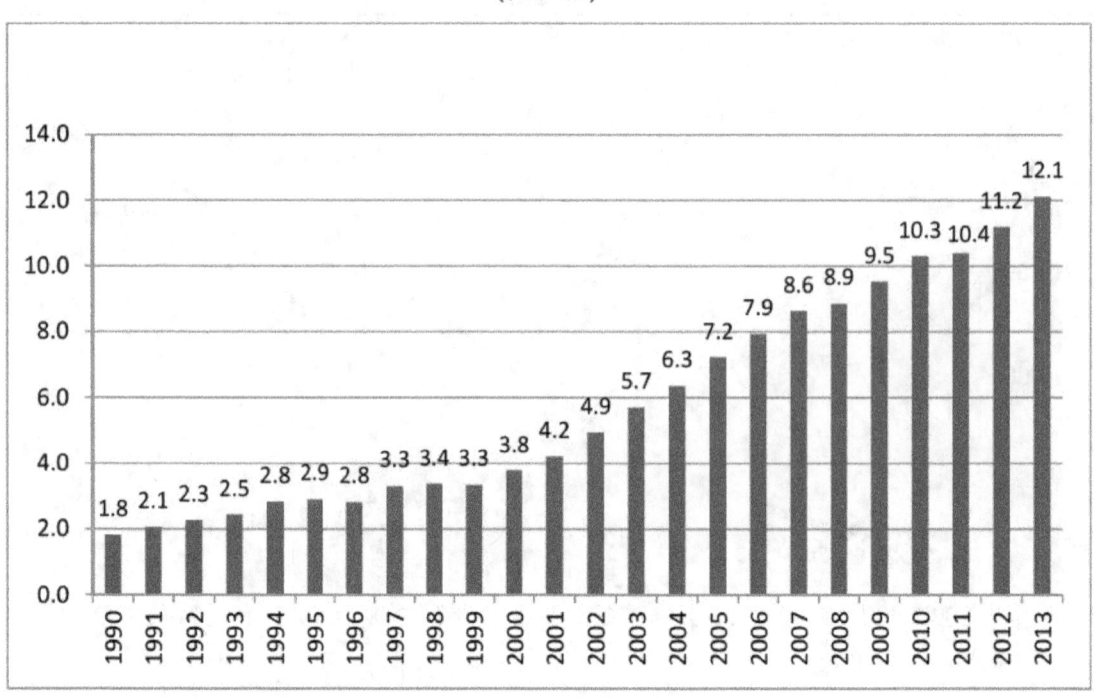

**Source:** Economist Intelligence Unit.

## China's Major Trading Partners

**Table 5** lists official Chinese trade data on its major trading partners in 2013 (based on total trade), which included the 28 countries that make up the European Union (EU28), the United States, the 10 nations that constitute the Association of Southeast Asian Nations (ASEAN), and Japan.[43] China's top three export markets were the Hong Kong, United States, and the EU28 while its top sources for imports were the EU28, ASEAN, and South Korea. According to Chinese data, it maintained large trade surpluses with Hong Kong ($369 billion), the United States ($222 billion), and the EU28 ($119 billion), and reported large trade imbalances with Taiwan (-$116 billion) and South Korea (-$92 billion). China's trade data differ significantly from those of many of its trading partners. These differences appear to be largely caused by how China's trade via Hong Kong is counted in official Chinese trade data. China treats a large share of its exports through Hong Kong as Chinese exports to Hong Kong for statistical purposes, while many countries that import Chinese products through Hong Kong generally attribute their origin to China for statistical purposes, including the United States.[44]

---

[43] ASEAN members include Brunei, Cambodia, Indonesia, Laos, Malaysia, Myanmar (Burma), the Philippines, Singapore, Thailand, and Vietnam.

[44] See CRS Report RS22640, *What's the Difference?—Comparing U.S. and Chinese Trade Data*, by Michael F. Martin.

### Table 5. China's Major Trading Partners in 2013

($ billions)

| Country | Total Trade | Chinese Exports | Chinese Imports | China's Trade Balance |
|---|---|---|---|---|
| European Union | 559 | 339 | 220 | 119 |
| United States | 514 | 368 | 146 | 222 |
| ASEAN | 443 | 244 | 199 | 45 |
| Hong Kong | 401 | 385 | 16 | 369 |
| Japan | 312 | 150 | 162 | -12 |
| South Korea | 274 | 91 | 183 | -92 |
| Taiwan | 198 | 41 | 157 | -116 |
| **Total Chinese Trade** | **4,160** | **2,211** | **1,949** | **262** |

**Sources:** *Global Trade Atlas* and *World Trade Atlas.*

**Note:** Rankings according to China's total trade in 2013. China's bilateral trade data often differ substantially from that of its trading partners.

## Major Chinese Trade Commodities

China's abundance of low-cost labor has made it internationally competitive in many low-cost, labor-intensive manufactures. As a result, manufactured products constitute a significant share of China's trade. A substantial amount of China's imports is comprised of parts and components that are assembled into finished products, such as consumer electronic products and computers, and then exported. Often, the value-added to such products in China by Chinese workers is relatively small compared to the total value of the product when it is shipped abroad.

China's top 10 exports and imports in 2013 are listed in **Table 6** and **Table 7**, respectively, using the harmonized tariff system (HTS) on a two-digit level. Major exports included electrical machinery,[45] machinery (including computers), knit apparel, and furniture and bedding while major imports included electrical machinery, mineral fuel, machinery, and ores.

### Table 6. Major Chinese Exports: 2013

($ billions)

| HS Code | Description | $ billions | Percent of Total | 2012/2011 % Change |
|---|---|---|---|---|
| | World | 2,211 | 100.0 | 7.8 |
| 85 | Electrical machinery | 562 | 25.4 | 15.2 |
| 84 | Machinery | 383 | 17.3 | 1.9 |
| 61 | Knit apparel | 97 | 4.4 | 11.2 |

---

[45] This includes electrical machinery and equipment and parts thereof; sound recorders and reproducers, television image and sound recorders and reproducers, and parts and accessories of such articles.

| HS Code | Description | $ billions | Percent of Total | 2012/2011 % Change |
|---|---|---|---|---|
| 94 | Furniture and bedding | 86 | 3.9 | 11.0 |
| 90 | Optical, photographic, cinematographic, measuring checking, precision, medical or surgical instruments and apparatus; parts and accessories thereof | 75 | 3.4 | 2.6 |
| 62 | Woven apparel | 68 | 3.1 | 11.5 |
| 39 | Plastics | 62 | 2.8 | 11.7 |
| 87 | Vehicles, except railway (mainly auto parts, motorcycles, trucks, and bicycles) | 59 | 2.7 | 6.2 |
| 73 | Iron and steel products | 57 | 2.6 | 2.1 |
| 64 | Footwear | 51 | 2.3 | 8.4 |

**Source:** *World Trade Atlas*, using official Chinese statistics.

**Notes:** Top 10 exports in 2013, two-digit level, harmonized tariff system.

### Table 7. Major Chinese Imports: 2013

($ billions)

| HS Code | Description | $ billions | Percent of Total | 2012/2011 % change |
|---|---|---|---|---|
| | World | 1,949 | 100.0 | 7.3 |
| 85 | Electrical machinery | 439 | 22.5 | 15.1 |
| 27 | Mineral fuel, oil etc. | 314 | 16.1 | 0.9 |
| 84 | Machinery | 171 | 8.8 | -6.2 |
| 26 | Ores, slag, and ash | 148 | 7.6 | 10.9 |
| 90 | Optical, photographic, cinematographic, measuring, checking, precision, medical or surgical instruments and apparatus; parts and accessories thereof | 108 | 5.5 | 1.3 |
| 98 | Special Classification | 105 | 5.4 | 52.3 |
| 87 | Vehicles, not railway (mainly autos and parts) | 74 | 3.8 | 5.0 |
| 39 | Plastics | 72 | 3.7 | 4.2 |
| 29 | Organic chemicals | 66 | 3.4 | 8.3 |
| 74 | Copper and articles thereof | 50 | 2.6 | -7.7 |

**Source:** *World Trade Atlas*, using official Chinese statistics.

**Notes:** Top 10 imports in 2013, two-digit level, harmonized tariff schedule.

## China's Growing Appetite for Energy

China's rapid economic growth has fueled a growing demand for energy, such as petroleum and coal, and that demand is becoming an increasingly important factor in determining global energy prices. According to the International Energy Agency (IEA), China overtook the United States in 2009 as the world's largest energy user (in comparison, China's energy use was only half that of that of the United States in 2000). According to the U.S. Energy Information Administration

(EIA), China's oil consumption growth accounted for half of the world's oil consumption growth in 2011.[46] According to IEA projections, China's demand for energy from 2008 (the baseline year) to 2035 will account for 30% of the projected increase in global demand for energy during this period. By 2035, China is projected to consume 70% more energy than the United States (even though, on a per capita basis, China's energy consumption will be less than half of U.S. levels).[47]

China is the world's second-largest consumer of oil products (after the United States) at 10.7 million barrels per day (bpd) in 2013, and that level is projected to rise to 16.9 million bpd by 2035.[48] China became a net oil importer (i.e., imports minus exports) in 1993. Net oil imports grew from 632,000 bpd in 1997 to 5.8 million bpd in 2013 (see **Figure 15**), making it the world's second-largest net oil importer after the United States.[49] In August 2013, the U.S. Energy Information Administration (EIA) projected that China would become the world's largest net importer by October 2013. By 2035, China's net oil imports per day are projected to exceed 13 million bpd.[50]

**Figure 15. China's Net Oil Imports: 1997-2013**

(millions of barrels per day)

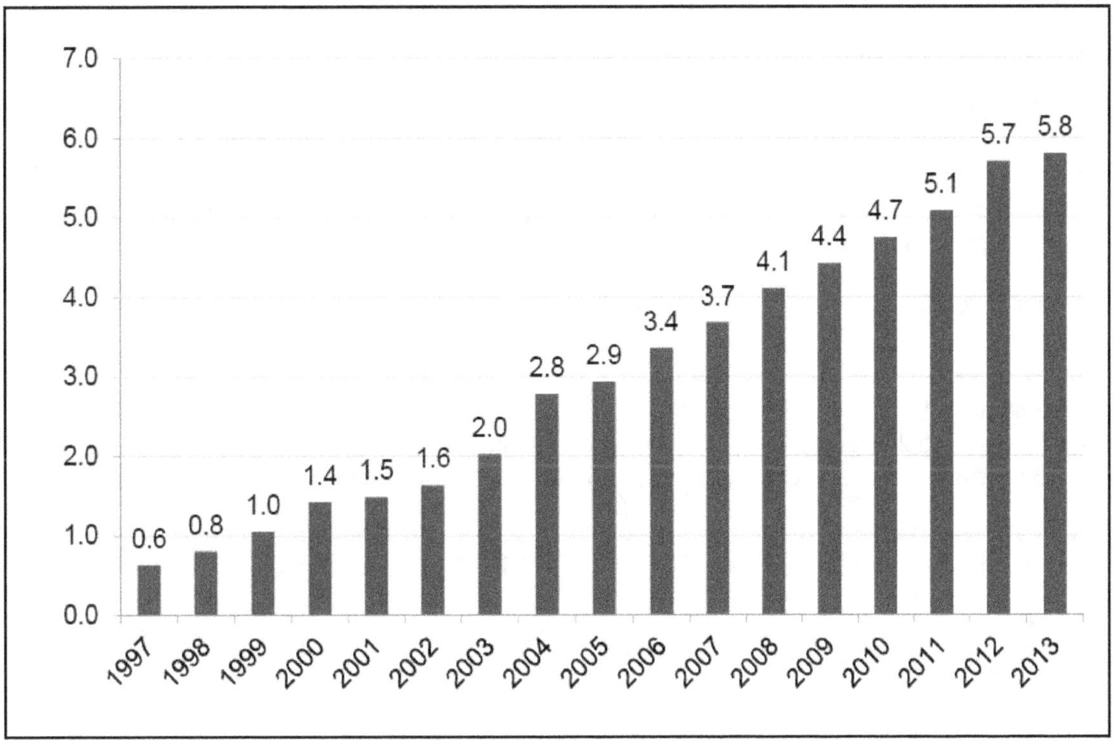

**Source:** U.S. Energy Administration and China Daily.

---

[46] EIA, Country Analysis Brief, China, September 2012, at http://www.eia.gov/countries/cab.cfm?fips=CH.

[47] International Energy Agency, *2012 World Energy Outlook*, November 2012, available at http://www.iea.org/.

[48] U.S. Energy Information Administration, *Forecasts and Analysis*, at http://www.eia.doe.gov/oiaf/forecasting.html.

[49] China overtook Japan as the second-largest net oil importer in 2009.

[50] EIA, *International Energy Outlook*, September 19, 2011, available at http://www.eia.gov/forecasts/ieo.

## China's Regional and Bilateral Free Trade Agreements

The Chinese government has maintained an active policy of boosting trade and investment ties around the world, especially with countries in Asia. To that end, China has entered into a number of regional and bilateral trade agreements, or is in the process of doing so. China currently has free trade agreements (FTAs) with ASEAN, Chile, Costa Rica, Hong Kong, Macau, New Zealand, Pakistan, Peru, and Singapore. China also has an "economic cooperation framework agreement" (ECFA) with Taiwan. China is currently in the process of negotiating FTAs with the Cooperation Council for the Arab States of the Gulf (which includes Saudi Arabia, Kuwait, the United Arab Emirates, Qatar, and Bahrain), Australia, Iceland, Norway, Switzerland, and the Southern African Customs Union (which includes South Africa, Botswana, Lesotho, Namibia, and Swaziland). In May 2012, China, Japan, and South Korea agreed to begin negotiations for an FTA in 2012. China has also considered negotiating an FTA with India, but with little progress to date.[51] In December 2012, China joined with the 10 members of ASEAN, Japan, South Korea, Australia, and New Zealand in agreement to begin negotiations toward a Regional Comprehensive Economic Partnership (RCEP), which, if concluded, could constitute the world's largest free trade bloc.[52]

# Major Long-Term Challenges Facing the Chinese Economy

China's economy has shown remarkable growth over the past several years, and many economists project that it will enjoy fairly healthy growth in the near future. However, economists caution that these projections are likely to occur only if China continues to make major reforms to its economy. Failure to implement such reforms could endanger future growth. They note that China's current economic model has resulted in a number of negative economic (and social) outcomes, such as over-reliance on fixed investment and exporting for its economic growth, extensive inefficiencies that exist in many sectors (due largely to government industrial policies), wide-spread pollution, and growing income inequality, to name a few. Many of China's economic problems and challenges stem from its incomplete transition to a free market economy and from imbalances that have resulted from the government's goal of economic growth at all costs.

## China's Incomplete Transition to a Market Economy

Despite China's three-decade history of widespread economic reforms, Chinese officials contend that China is a "socialist-market economy." This appears to indicate that the government accepts and allows the use of free market forces in a number of areas to help grow the economy, but the government still plays a major role in the country's economic development.

---

[51] Chinese Ministry of Commerce, *China FTA Network*, available at http://fta.mofcom.gov.cn/english/ fta_qianshu.shtml.

[52] The RCEP would include more than 3 billion people, have a combined GDP of $17 trillion

## Industrial Policies and SOEs

According to the World Bank, "China has become one of the world's most active users of industrial policies and administrations."[53] According to one estimate, China's SOEs may account for up of 50% of non-agriculture GDP.[54] In addition, although the number of SOEs has declined sharply, they continue to dominate a number of sectors (such as petroleum and mining, telecommunications, utilities, transportation, and various industrial sectors); are shielded from competition; are the main sectors encouraged to invest overseas; and dominate the listings on China's stock indexes.[55] One study found that SOEs constituted 50% of the 500 largest manufacturing companies in China and 61% of the top 500 service sector enterprises.[56] It is estimated that there were 154,000 SOEs as of 2008, and while these accounted for only 3.1% of all enterprises in China, they held 30% of the value of corporate assets in the manufacturing and services sectors.[57] Of the 58 Chinese firms on the 2011 *Fortune* Global 500 list, 54 were identified as having government ownership of 50% or more.[58] The World Bank estimates that more than one in four SOEs lose money.[59]

## The Banking System

China's banking system is largely controlled by the central government, which attempts to ensure that capital (credit) flows to industries deemed by the government to be essential to China's economic development. SOEs are believed to receive preferential credit treatment by government banks, while private firms must often pay higher interest rates or obtain credit elsewhere. According to one estimate, SOEs accounted for 85% ($1.4 trillion) of all bank loans in 2009.[60] In addition, the government sets interest rates for depositors at very low rates, often below the rate of inflation, which keeps the price of capital relatively low for firms.[61] It is believed that oftentimes SOEs do not repay their loans, which may have saddled the banks with a large amount of nonperforming loans. In addition, local governments are believed to have borrowed extensively from state banks shortly after the global economic slowdown began to impact the Chinese economy to fund infrastructure and other initiatives. Some contend these measures could further add to the amount of nonperforming loans held by the banks. Many analysts contend that

---

[53] The World Bank, *China:2030*, p. 114.

[54] U.S.-China Economic and Security Review Commission, An Analysis of State-owned Enterprises and State Capitalism in China, by Andrew Szamosszegi and Cole Kyle, October 26, 2011, p.1.

[55] The nature of China's SOEs has become increasing complex. Many SOEs appear to be run like private companies. For example, and a number of SOEs have made initial public offerings in China's stock markets and those in other countries (including the United States), although the Chinese government is usually the largest shareholder. It is not clear to what extent the Chinese government attempts to influence decisions made by the SOE's which have become shareholding companies.

[56] Xiao Geng, Xiuke Yang, and Anna Janus, *State-owned Enterprises in China, Reform Dynamics and Impacts*, 2009, p.155.

[57] The World Bank, *State-Owned Enterprises in China: How Big Are They?*, January 19, 2010.

[58] Global 500, The World's Largest Corporations," *Fortune*, July 25, 2011, available at http://money.cnn.com/magazines/fortune/global500/2011/index html.

[59] World Bank, *China 2030*, p.25.

[60] The Economist, *State Capitalism's Global Reach, New Masters of the Universe, How State Enterprise is Spreading*, January 21, 2012, available at http://www.economist.com/node/21542925.

[61] Some economists argue that a significant portion of China's SOEs could not stay in business if they had to pay a market-based interest rate for credit.

one of the biggest weaknesses of the banking system is that it lacks the ability to ration and allocate credit according to market principles, such as risk assessment.

Local government debt is viewed as a growing problem in China, largely because of the potential impact it could have on the Chinese banking system. During the beginning of the global financial slowdown, many Chinese subnational government entities borrowed extensively to help stimulate local economies, especially by supporting infrastructure projects. In December 2013, the Chinese National Audit Office reported that from the end of 2010 to mid-year 2013, local government debt had increased by 67% to nearly $3 trillion.[62]

## An Undervalued Currency

China does not allow its currency to float and therefore must make large-scale purchases of dollars to keep the exchange rate within certain target levels. Although the renminbi (RMB) has appreciated against the dollar in real terms by about 40% since reforms were introduced in July 2005, some analysts contend that it remains highly undervalued.[63] China's undervalued currency makes its exports less expensive, and its imports more expensive, than would occur under a floating exchange rate system. In order to maintain its exchange rate target, the government must purchase foreign currency (such as the dollar) by expanding the money supply. This makes it much more difficult for the government to use monetary policy to combat inflation.[64]

Many economists argue that China's industrial policies have sharply limited competition and the growth of the private sector, caused over-capacity in many industries, and distorted markets by artificially lowering the costs of various factor costs (such as capital, water, land, and energy) below market levels in order to promote targeted industrial sectors. Such policies have come at the expense of other (non-industrial) sectors of the economy, such as services.

## Overdependence on Exporting and Fixed Investment

A 2009 IMF reported estimated that fixed investment related to tradable goods plus net exports together accounted for over 60% of China's GDP growth from 2001 to 2008 (up from 40% from 1990 to 2000), which was significantly higher than in the G-7 countries (16%), the euro area (30%), and the rest of Asia (35%).[65] As indicated in **Figure 16**, from 1990 to 2013, Chinese gross savings as a percent of GDP and gross fixed investment as a percent of GDP both increased significantly, while private consumption as a percent of GDP declined sharply. In addition, as indicated in **Figure 17**, personal disposable income in China as a share of GDP was lower in 2013

---

[62] The Wall Street Journal, *Xi Faces Test over China's Local Debt; Risks From Debt are Still Controllable, Audit Office Says*, December 30, 2013.

[63] See CRS Report RS21625, *China's Currency Policy: An Analysis of the Economic Issues*, by Wayne M. Morrison and Marc Labonte.

[64] If Chinese banks raised interest rates in an effort to control inflation, overseas investors might to try to shift funds to China (through illegal means) to take advantage of the higher Chinese rates. The Chinese government has had difficulty blocking such inflows of "hot money." Such inflows force the government to boost the money supply to buy up the foreign currency necessary to maintain the targeted peg. Expanding the money supply contributes to easy credit policies by the banks, which has contributed to overcapacity in a number of sectors, such as steel, and speculative asset bubbles (such as in real estate). This often forces the government to use administrative controls to limit credit to certain sectors.

[65] Guo, Kai and Papa N'Diaye, *Is China's Export-Oriented Growth Sustainable*, IMF Working Paper, August 2009

---

(43.9%) than it was in 2000 (47.9%).[66] China's gross savings as a percent of GDP and gross fixed investment as a percent of GDP are the highest among any of the world's largest economies, while China's private consumption as a share of GDP is the lowest.[67]

Many economists contend that the falling share of private consumption and disposable income relative to GDP is largely caused by two main factors: China's banking policies and the lack of an adequate social safety net. The Chinese government places restrictions on the export of capital. As a result, Chinese households put a large share of their savings in domestic banks. The Chinese government sets the interest rate on deposits. Often this rate is below the rate of inflation, which lowers household income. Some economists consider this policy to constitute a transfer of wealth from Chinese households to Chinese firms which benefit from low interest rates. This "tax" on household income negatively affects household consumption. Secondly, China's lack of an adequate social safety net (such as pensions, health care, unemployment insurance, and education) induces households to save a large portion of their income. According to one estimate, the average saving rate of urban households relative to their disposable incomes rose from 18% in 1995 to nearly 29% in 2009.[68] Corporations are also a major contributor to the high savings rate in China. Many Chinese firms, especially SOEs, do not pay out dividends and thus are able to retain most of their earnings. Many economists contend that requiring the SOEs to pay dividends could boost private consumption in China.

Chinese economic policies have resulted in gross fixed investment being the main engine of the country's economic growth for every year from 2000 to 2013 (In 2011 gross fixed investment and private consumptions each accounted for 3.0 percentage points) (see **Figure 16**).[69]

---

[66] Source: Economist Intelligence Unit.

[67] Chinese private consumption as a percent of GDP in 2013 was 36.4%. Rates for other countries include the United States (at 68.3%), Brazil (62.9%), Japan (61.4%), Germany (57.6%), India (56.1%), and Russia (51.3%). Source: EIU.

[68] VOX, *The Puzzle of China's Rising Household Saving Rate*, by Marcos Chamon, Kai Liu, and Eswar Prasad, January 18, 2011, available at http://voxeu.org/index.php?q=node/6028.

[69] The last time private consumption was the largest contributor to GDP was 1999.

### Figure 16. Chinese Gross Savings, Gross Fixed Investment, and Private Consumption as a Percent of GDP: 1990-2013

(percent)

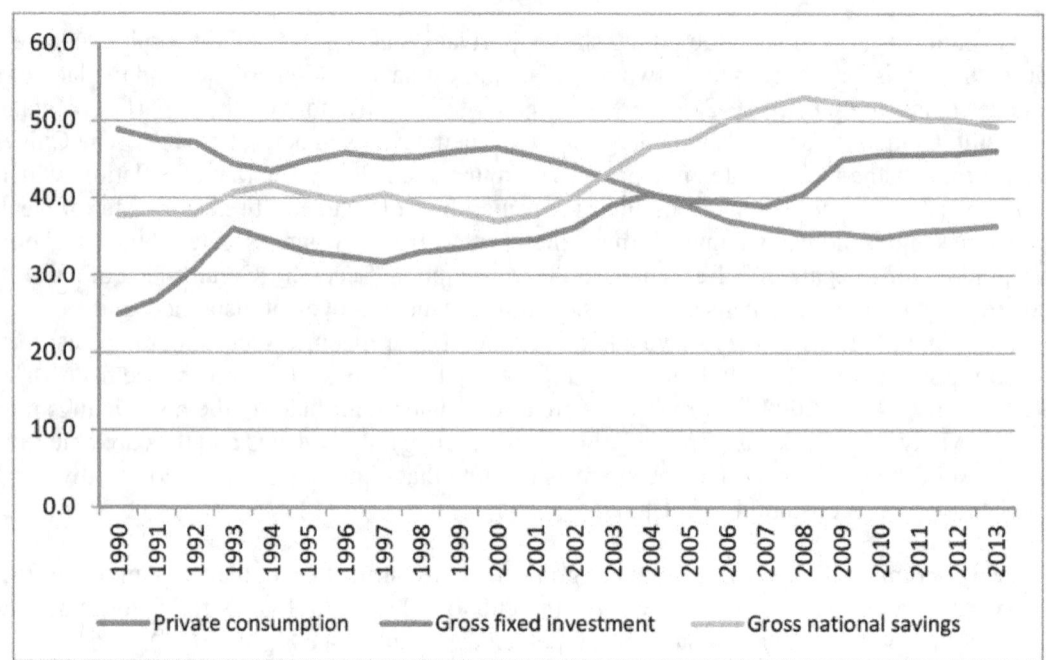

Source: Economist Intelligence Unit.

### Figure 17. Chinese Disposable Personal Income as a Percent of GDP: 2000-2013

(percent)

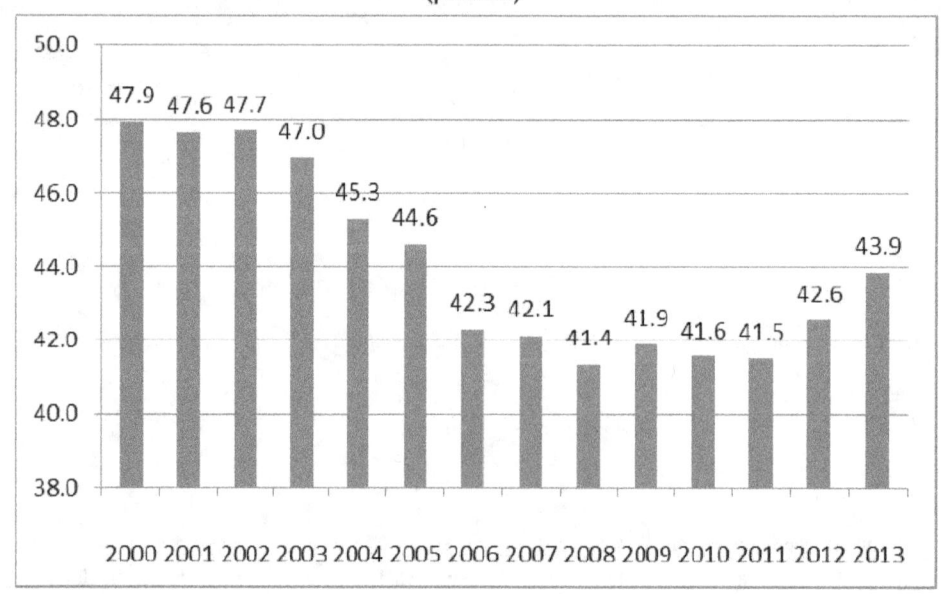

Source: Economist Intelligence Unit.

Note: Data for 2013 are estimates.

**Figure 18. Sources of Chinese GDP Growth: 2007-2013**

(percentage points)

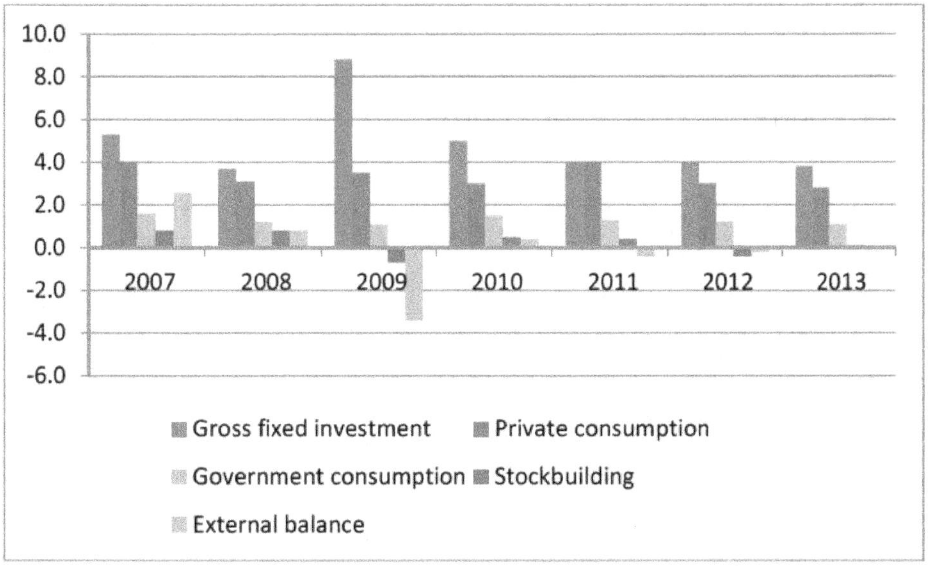

**Source:** Economist Intelligence Unit.

**Notes:** Real GDP growth rates for 2007-2013 were as follows: 14.2% in 2007, 9.6% in 2008, 9.2% in 2009, 10.4% in 2010, 9.2% in 2011, and 7.7% in both 2012 and 2013.

## Growing Pollution

China's economic growth model has emphasized the growth of heavy industry in China, much of which is energy-intensive and high polluting. The level of pollution in China continues to worsen, posing serious health risks to the population. The Chinese government often disregards its own environmental laws in order to promote rapid economic growth. China's environmental challenges are illustrated by the following incidents and reports:

- The U.S. Embassy in Beijing, which monitors and reports air quality in China based on an air quality index of particle matter (developed by the U.S. Environmental Protection Agency) considered to pose a health concern, reported that the air quality in Beijing for a majority of the days in January 2013 ranged from "unhealthy" to "hazardous" (based on 24-hour exposure) and, on a few days, it recorded high readings that were "beyond index."[70] The level of poor air quality in Beijing was termed by some in China as "Airpocalypse," and reportedly forced the government to shut down some factories and reduce the level of official cars on the road.[71] On December 9, 2013, China's media reported that half of China was blanketed by smog.[72] The U.S. Consulate General in Shanghai reported that were a number of days in December 2013 where its

---

[70] Hazardous is the worst category for air quality used by the U.S. embassy, based on a numerical value of its index ranging from 301 to 500. A measurement of below 50 is considered good. On several occasions, the air quality index in Beijing has surpassed 500 and on January 12, 2013, it reportedly hit 755.

[71] National Public Radio, *Beijing's "Airpocalypse" Spurs Pollution Controls, Public Pressure*, January 14, 2013.

[72] Xinhua, December 9, 2013.

measurement of the air quality in Shanghai was hazardous or very unhealthy, and during some time periods on December 5, 2013, its readings were "beyond index."

- In February 2013, China's Geological Survey reportedly estimated that 90% of all Chinese cities had polluted groundwater, with two-thirds having "severely polluted" water.[73]

- According to a 2012 report by the Asian Development Bank, less than 1% of the 500 largest cities in China meet the air quality standards recommended by the World Health Organization, and 7 of these are ranked among the 10 most polluted cities in the world.[74]

- The U.S. Entergy Information Administration (EIA) projected in 2011 that by 2035, China's carbon dioxide emissions ($CO_2$) could be nearly double its current levels.[75] A study by ExxonMobil projects that, by 2030, China's $CO_2$ emissions could equal the level in the United States and EU combined.[76]

- The World Health Organization estimated that air pollution in China caused the death of 470,649 people in 2008.[77]

The Chinese government has sharply criticized foreign governments for reporting air quality in China, calling their readings inaccurate and complaining that releasing such data violates international conventions and Chinese laws.[78] At the same time, China's media has boosted its reporting of China's environmental problems in response to public anger, prompting central government officials to promise new steps to reduce emissions. However, the central government has often found it difficult to induce SOEs and local governments to comply with environmental laws, especially when such officials feel doing so will come at the expense of economic growth.

## Corruption and the Relative Lack of the Rule of Law

The relative lack of the rule of law in China has led to widespread government corruption, financial speculation, and misallocation of investment funds. In many cases, government "connections," not market forces, are the main determinant of successful firms in China. Many U.S. firms find it difficult to do business in China because rules and regulations are generally not consistent or transparent, contracts are not easily enforced, and intellectual property rights are not protected (due to the lack of an independent judicial system). The relative lack of the rule of law and widespread government corruption in China limit competition and undermine the efficient allocation of goods and services in the economy. A *New York Times* article reported that (former) Chinese Premier Wen Jiabao's family controlled assets worth at least $2.7 billion.[79] One study estimates that between 2001 and 2010, China was the world's largest source of illicit capital

---

[73] *The New York Times, Concerns Grow About 'Severely Polluted' Water in China's Cities*, February 20, 2013.

[74] The Asian Development Bank, *Toward an Environmentally Sustainable Future, Country Environmental Analysis of the People's Republic of China*, 2012, p. xviii.

[75] EIA, International Energy Outlook, September 19, 2011, available at http://www.eia.gov/forecasts/ieo.

[76] ExxonMobil, *The Outlook for Energy*, A View to 2030, December 29, 2009, p. 4.

[77] World Health Organization chart at http://gamapserver.who.int/gho/interactive_charts/phe/oap_mbd/atlas.html.

[78] See Xinhua, Foreign Embassies' Air Data Issuing Inaccurate, Unlawful: Official, June 5, 2012, at http://news.xinhuanet.com/english/china/2012-06/05/c_131633044.htm

[79] *The New York Times*, Billions in Hidden Riches for Family of Chinese Leader, October 25, 2012.

outflows at $3.8 trillion.[80] A 2012 survey by the Pew Research Center's Global Attitudes Project reported that 50% of respondents said that corrupt officials are a very big problem (up from 39% in 2008).[81] Chinese officials often identify government corruption as the greatest threat to the Chinese Communist Party and the state. The Chinese government's anti-corruption watchdog reported that 106,000 officials were found guilty of corruption in 2009.[82] However, many analysts contend that government anti-corruption campaigns are mainly used to settle political scores with out of favor officials and argue that meaningful progress against government corruption cannot occur without greater government transparency, a system of checks and balances, a free press, and an independent judiciary.[83]

China maintains a weak and relatively decentralized government structure to regulate economic activity in China. Laws and regulations often go unenforced or are ignored by local government officials. As a result, many firms cut corners in order to maximize profits. This has led to a proliferation of unsafe food and consumer products being sold in China or exported abroad. Lack of government enforcement of food safety laws led to a massive recall of melamine-tainted infant milk formula that reportedly killed at least four children and sickened 53,000 others in 2008.

# Plans Announced by the Chinese Government to Reform and Restructure the Economy

Various government officials have publicly stated the need for China to change course from its traditional economic growth model of growth at all cost to one that balances economic growth with a number of social goals in order to develop a "socialist harmonious society," and to further modernize the economy. In March 2007, Chinese Premier Wen Jiabao stated that there are "structural problems in China's economy which cause unsteady, unbalanced, uncoordinated and unsustainable development." He defined "unsteady development" as overheated investment, excessive credit and liquidity, and merchandise trade and current account surpluses. "Unbalanced development" was described as economic disparities between rural and urban areas, regions of the country, and between economic and social development. "Uncoordinated development" was described as the lack of balance between various sectors of the economy (especially in regards to the services sector) and between investment and consumption (i.e., economic growth is mainly driven by investment and exports rather than consumer demand). Lastly, "unsustainable development" referred to problems caused by China's inefficient use of energy and resources and failure to protect the environment.

## The Central Government Five-Year Plans

China's last two five-year plans (FYP), the 11th FYP (2006-2010) and the 12th FYP (2011-2015), have placed strong emphasis on promoting consumer demand, addressing income disparities

---

[80] Global Financial Integrity, *Chinese Economy Lost $3.79 Trillion in Illicit Financial Outflows Since 2000, Reveals New GFI Report*, October 25, 2012. It is not known how much of the illicit financial outflows in China are directly linked to government corruption.

[81] Pew Research Global Attitudes Project, *Growing Concerns in China about Inequality, Corruption*, October 16, 2012.

[82] BBC News, *Corruption Up Among China Government Officials*, January 8, 2010.

[83] *The New York Times, Chinese Officials Find Misbehavior Now Carries Cost*, December 25, 2012.

(such as by boosting spending on social safety net programs), boosting energy efficiency, reducing pollution, improving the rule of law, and deepening economic reforms. Those plans have also identified a number of industries and technologies that the government has targeted for development (see text box).

---

### China's 12th Five-Year Plan[84]

China's Five-Year Plans (FYPs) have been issued by the government since 1953. The FYP is the major vehicle for the government to establish broad economic and social goals for the time period under consideration, to coordinate investments between the central and local governments, and to oversee implementation of policy. Not only does the plan influence investments by government entities, it also provides direction for bank lending and government approvals and regulation of private and semi-private industries. In March 2011, China's National People's Congress approved the 12th Five-Year Plan (covering the years 2011 to 2015).

The 12th FYP (2011-2015) contains three broad themes or areas of focus: (1) economic restructuring, (2) promoting greater social equality, and (3) protecting the environment. Chinese industrial policy comes into play primarily in economic restructuring but also is apparent in the other areas of focus. Particularly noteworthy is the targeting of seven strategic emerging industries that are intended to become the backbone of China's economy in the future and to be able to compete well on a global scale. These seven industries are (1) biotechnology; (2) new energy; (3) high-end equipment manufacturing; (4) energy conservation and environmental protection; (5) clean-energy vehicles; (6) new materials; and (7) next-generation information technology. The government reportedly intends to spend up to $2.1 trillion on these industries during the 12th FYP. Some of the highlights of the FYP include:

- Achieving an average real GDP growth rate of 7% and ensuring that incomes rise at least as fast as GDP;

- Consolidating inefficient sectors and promoting the services industry (with the goal of expanding service sector output to account for 47% of GDP—up four percentage points from the current level);

- Promoting energy saving and new energy industries; promoting the development of nuclear, water, wind, and solar power; and expanding non-fossil fuel to account for 11.4% of primary energy consumption;

- Welcoming foreign investment in modern agriculture, high-technology, and environmental protection industries;

- Turning coastal regions from "world's factory" to hubs of research and development, high-end manufacturing, and services;

- Lengthening high-speed railway and highway networks;

- Increasing expenditure on R&D to account for 2.2% of GDP;

- Expanding non-fossil fuel to account for 11.4% of primary energy consumption;

- Cutting water consumption per unit of value-added industrial output by 30%, energy consumption per unit of GDP by 16%, and carbon dioxide emission per unit of GDP by 17%;

- Increasing the minimum wage by no less than 13% on average each year; and

- Building 36 million affordable apartments for low-income people.

**Sources:** Xinhua News Agency, *Highlights of China's 12th Five-Year Plan*, March 5, 2011; and APCO Worldwide, *China's 12th Five-Year Plan: How it Actually Works and What's in Store For the Next Five Years*, December 10, 2010.

---

## The Drive for "Indigenous Innovation"

Many of the industrial policies that China has implemented or formulated since 2006 appear to stem largely from a comprehensive document issued by China's State Council (the highest executive organ of state power) in 1996 titled *The National Medium-and Long-Term Program for Science and Technology Development (2006-2020)*, often referred to as the MLP. The MLP

---

[84] "Highlights of China's Draft 12th Five-Year Plan," *Xinhua*, March 5, 2011.

appears to represent an ambitious plan to modernize the structure of China's economy by transforming it from a global center of low-tech manufacturing to a major center of innovation (by the year 2020) and a global innovation leader by 2050. As some observers describe it, China wants to go from a model of "made in China" to "innovated in China." It also seeks to sharply reduce the country's dependence on foreign technology. The MLP includes the stated goals of "indigenous innovation, leapfrogging in priority fields, enabling development, and leading the future."[85] Some of the broad goals of the MLP state that by 2020:

- The progress of science and technology will contribute 60% or above to China's development.

- The country's reliance on foreign technology will decline to 30% or below (from an estimated current level of 50%).

- Gross expenditures for research and development (R&D) would rise to 2.5% of gross domestic product (from 1.3% in 2005). Priority areas for increased R&D include space programs, aerospace development and manufacturing, renewable energy, computer science, and life sciences.[86]

The document states that "China must place the strengthening of indigenous innovative capability at the core of economic restructuring, growth model change, and national competitiveness enhancement. Building an innovation-oriented country is therefore a major strategic choice for China's future development." This goal, according to the document, is to be achieved by formulating and implementing regulations in the country's government procurement law to "encourage and protect indigenous innovation," establishing a coordination mechanism for government procurement of indigenous innovative products, requiring a first-buy policy for major domestically made high-tech equipment and products that possess proprietary intellectual property rights, providing policy support to enterprises in procuring domestic high-tech equipment, and developing "relevant technology standards" through government procurement.

## Economic Policies Outlined in the November 2013 Third Plenum

From November 9-12, 2013, the Communist Party of China held the Third Plenum of its 18th Party Congress, a meeting that many analysts anticipated would result in the initiation of extensive new economic reforms under China's new leadership. Following the meeting, the Communist Party issued a communique with a number of broad (and often vague) policy statements on reforms to be implemented by 2020, and then a few days later it issued a 60-point document that provided more detail of the Plenum's results. Many of the proposed reforms addressed issues to boost competition and economic efficiency. The Plenum also established a new "Central Leading Group" to design and coordinate the proposed reforms.

One of the major results of the Plenum highlighted by the Chinese media was that the market would now play a "decisive" role in allocating resources in the economy. China's media stated the economic reforms announced in the communique were comparable to those announced in 1978,

---

[85] The MLP identifies main areas and priority topics, including energy, water and mineral resources, the environment, agriculture, manufacturing, communications and transport, information industry and modern service industries, population and health, urbanization and urban development, public security, and national defense. The report also identifies 16 major special projects and 8 "pioneer technologies."

[86] *R&D Magazine*, December 22, 2009.

when major reforms were first undertaken, and in 1992, when the Communist party agreed that the market should be the "basic" means of allocating resources under the concept of a socialist market economy. The 2013 Plenum communique thus elevated markets from having a "basic" role in resource allocation to having a "decisive" role.[87] It further stated that "both public and non-public ownership are key components of China's socialist market economy."

While appearing to elevate the role of the private sector in the economy, the Plenum communique also emphasized the importance of the public sector in the economy, stating that China "must unwaveringly consolidate and develop the publicly owned economy, persist in the dominant role of the public ownership system, give rein to the leading role of the State-owned economy, and incessantly strengthen the vitality, control, strength and influence of the State-owned economy." Some observers contend that this could indicate that the Chinese government will continue to actively support and protect state-owned enterprises (SOEs). Others argue that the Plenum documents indicate that SOEs will be subject to structural and market-based reforms.

For example, the 60-point document indicates that China plans to push forward with market-based price reforms, including for water, oil, natural gas, electricity, transport, and telecommunications (sectors that generally been dominated by SOEs and used to subsidize other SOEs); allow nonpublic entities to invest in SOEs, and increase the level of dividends SOEs are required to transfer back to the government for use in social safety net programs. The document emphasizes the goals of perfecting a mechanism where prices are determined by the market; making market rules that are fair, open, and transparent; implementing a unified market entrance system where market players of all kind are allowed to compete (except in sectors on a "negative list"); reducing regional protectionism; and improving market exit mechanisms to promote the "survival of the fittest."

Other proposed areas of reforms include improving protection of intellectual property rights; implementing new financial reforms (such as allowing more private banks, improving market mechanisms for the exchange rate of the renminbi, and accelerating interest rate liberalization and capital account convertibility); liberalizing rules on foreign investment and establishing new free trade zones; and improving macroeconomic control over the economy while reducing government involvement in market operations.

The extent of China's economic reforms resulting from the meeting (and how they will be implemented) will not be fully understood until more information is made available by the Chinese government. As noted by U.S. Treasury Secretary Jacob Lew, who visited Beijing shortly after the Plenum: "I think there is going to continue to be progress, but the question is how much and how quickly."-

# Challenges to U.S. Policy of China's Economic Rise

China's rapid economic growth and emergence as a major economic power have given China's leadership increased confidence in its economic model. Many believe the key challenges for the

---

[87] For example, an editorial by Xinhua on November 13, 2013, stated that this was "not only a change in wording, but more importantly, a breakthrough in China's market reform and highlighting the importance of market power. The expression also means that the state should exert the government's role under the domination of the market, rather than exerting the market's role under the domination of the government."

United States are to convince China that (1) it has a stake in maintaining the international trading system, which is largely responsible for its economic rise, and to take a more active leadership role in maintaining that system; and (2) that further economic and trade reforms are the surest way for China to grow and modernize its economy. For example, by boosting domestic spending and allowing its currency to appreciate, China would import more, which would help speed economic recovery in other countries, promote more stable and balanced economic growth in China, and lessen trade protectionist pressures around the world. Lowering trade barriers on imports would boost competition in China, lower costs for consumers, and increase economic efficiency. However, many U.S. stakeholders are concerned that China's efforts to boost the development of indigenous innovation and technology could result in greater intervention by the state (such as subsidies, trade and investment barriers, and discriminatory policies), which could negatively affect U.S. IP-intensive firms. Failure by China to take meaningful steps to rebalance its economy could increase tensions with its trading partners, especially if China's share of global exports continues to increase rapidly, and if that increase is viewed as being the result of non-market policies that give Chinese exports an unfair competitive advantage.[88] Some economists contend that some economic rebalancing by China appears to have taken place in recent years, noting that China's current account surplus as a percent of GDP declined from a historical high of 10.1% in 2007 to 2.5% in 2013 (see **Figure 19**). In addition, private consumption as a percent of GDP has risen annually from 2011 to 2013. However, many economists contend that much of the reduction in China's current account surplus may largely the result of sluggish global demand for Chinese products, rather than a significant change in Chinese economic policies. In July 2012, the IMF stated that, although the fall of China's current account surplus was a welcome sign, the external rebalancing was achieved at the cost of rising internal imbalances—namely the high rate of investment spending, which, the IMF assessed, would be difficult to sustain.[89] In addition, gross fixed investment as a percent of GDP grew each year from 2011 to 2013, and continues to be the dominant source of China's GDP growth.

---

[88] Sharp increases in Chinese exports of higher-end manufacturing could also raise trade tensions between China and its major trading partners. This has already occurred in some areas, such as wind turbines and solar panels.

[89] IMF, *People's Republic of China: 2010 Article IV Consultation—Staff Report For the 2012 Article IV Consultation*, July 6, 2011, p. 1.

**Figure 19. Current Account Balances as a Percent of GDP for China
and the United States: 2000-2013**

(percent)

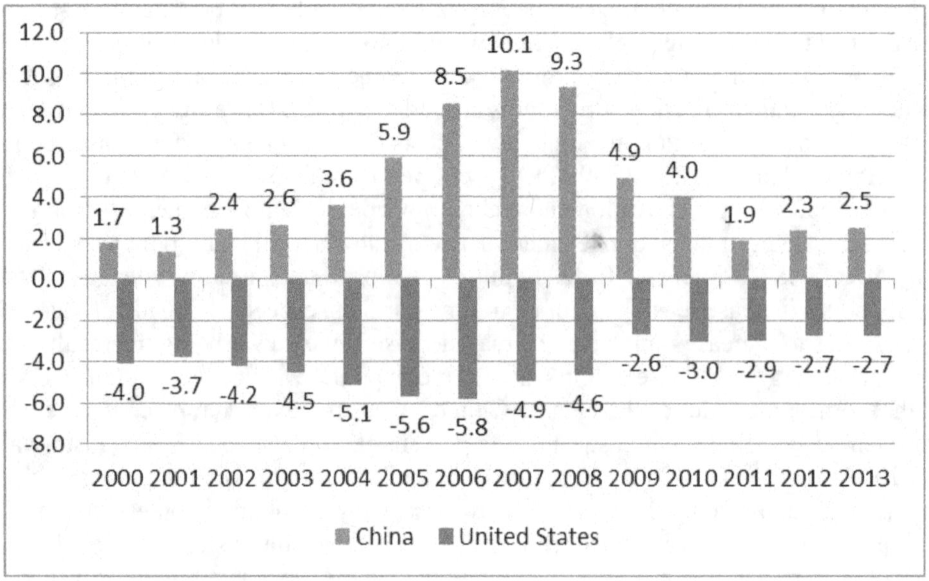

**Source:** International Monetary Fund.

**Note:** Data for 2013 are IMF estimates made in October 2013.

Opinions differ as to the most effective way of dealing with China on major economic issues. Some support a policy of engagement with China using various forums, such as the U.S.-China Strategic and Economic Dialogue (S&ED), which holds discussions on major long-term economic issues at the highest government level. Others support a somewhat mixed policy of using engagement when possible, coupled with a more aggressive use of the World Trade Organization (WTO) dispute settlement procedures to address China's unfair trade policies. Still others, who see China as a growing threat to the U.S. economy and the global trading system, advocate a policy of trying to contain China's economic power and using punitive measures when needed to force China to "play by the rules." Media reports of extensive cyber espionage by Chinese entities (including the Chinese military) against U.S. firms have also raised concern in the United States over how to respond what many see as a serious threat to U.S. economic interests.[90]

China's growing economic power has made it a critical and influential player on the global stage on a number of issues important to U.S. interests, such as global economic cooperation, climate change, nuclear proliferation, and North Korean aggression.[91] China is in a position to help advance U.S. interests or to frustrate them. China's rising economy has also enabled it to boost its military capabilities.

---

[90] For example, see Mandiant, *APT1, Exposing One of China's Cyber Espionage Units*, February 19, 2013. The report documents cyber espionage by a Chinese entity (believed to be linked to the Chinese People's Liberation) against more than 141 companies in 20 industries.

[91] For additional information on these issues, see CRS Report R41108, *U.S.-China Relations: An Overview of Policy Issues*, by Susan V. Lawrence.

U.S. policy makers face a number of complex challenges on how to deal with these issues. Can the United States compel better behavior from China via quiet diplomacy or public confrontation? Has U.S. leverage over Beijing lessened in the wake of China's economic rise, and has China's leverage over Washington increased? Are China's new leaders serious about undertaking comprehensive reforms as outlined in the Third Plenum?[92] Does Chinese President Xi Jinping have the power to implement new economic reforms if they are opposed by other factions of the government that have a stake in maintaining the status quo? To what extent will the Chinese government be willing to reduce or eliminate preferential policies (such as subsidies and preferential bank loans) given to SOEs? Will the reforms result in a significant reduction in trade and investment barriers against U.S. firms?

# Author Contact Information

Wayne M. Morrison
Specialist in Asian Trade and Finance
wmorrison@crs.loc.gov, 7-7767

---

[92] In March 2013, Xi Jinping formally replaced Hu Jintao as China's President (Xi is also general secretary of the Communist Party of China Central Committee). Many analysts argue that during the eight years of Hu's presidency, economic reforms in China were essentially stalled (and in some instances, reversed) compared to policies under the previous Chinese leader, President Jiang Zemin. On several occasions, China's media has reported President Xi call for deepening economic reforms, but few specific reforms been announced by the government to date.

www.ingramcontent.com/pod-product-compliance
Lightning Source LLC
Chambersburg PA
CBHW080632290526
45790CB00007B/3029